T0063545

"BLESSED THE MERCIFUL"

The CHESED-Oriented Christian Life

BENJAMIN A VIMA

Order this book online at www.trafford.com
or email orders@trafford.com

Most Trafford titles are also available at major online book retailers.

Print information available on the last page.

ISBN: 978-1-4907-7054-3 (sc)
ISBN: 978-1-4907-7055-0 (e)

Library of Congress Control Number: 2016902873

Trafford rev. 02/19/2016

   www.trafford.com

North America & international
toll-free: 1 888 232 4444 (USA & Canada)
fax: 812 355 4082

CONTENTS

DEDICATION

I gratefully dedicate this book to my friends who collaborated with me in establishing and managing the charitable agency Green Cross Ministries Inc. through which I have been trying to fulfill the CHESED Command of the Good Samaritan in feeding, sheltering, and liberating so many orphans and widows who are neglected and mistreated in their communities.

INTRODUCTION

A t the outset, I want my readers to get a clear understanding of this book's title, BLESSED THE MERCIFUL. It is taken from Jesus's Sermon on the Mount as told by Matthew in his Gospel. It is included as one of the nine beatitudes: "Blessed are the merciful, for they will be shown mercy." In his mind, Matthew upheld that mercy of God is more to be seen as forgiveness that comes from God as well as what we show to our fellowmen (Ref. 6:15; 18:35). Apostle James expounds it further by saying, "For the judgment is merciless to one who has not shown mercy; mercy triumphs over judgment" (James 2: 13).

Though Luke talks about Jesus's beatitudes in his Gospel (6) very admiringly, he offers little more positive and heavenly color to *mercy* as he writes Jesus, saying, "Be merciful, just as [also] your Father is merciful." Our Master wanted us to be merciful as our God is forever. Jesus demands from us a godly and very costly mercy. This is what I will be expounding in this book.

Undoubtedly in all NT books, *forgiveness* is the primary meaning thrust to the term *mercy*. Nonetheless, all of them never cease to proclaim mercy in its total fullness. In this book, I deal with the term *mercy* not simply as an isolated one referring to forgiveness that we receive from God and that we offer to our neighbors. I would contend that the meaning of *mercy* is greater than that.

Let us look at Matthew's approach. This scriptural verse is from the Gospel of Matthew, who was a converted public sinner of unjust tax collecting. After describing the baptism experience of Jesus (Matt. 3:13–17), during which Jesus was anointed by the Holy Spirit and he heard loudly his Father's voice who said, "This is my beloved Son with whom I am well pleased," Matthew narrates how the baptized and purified Jesus was led by the Spirit into the desert to be tempted by the devil. Victoriously defeating Satan's shrewd allurements, Jesus marches on his journey of proclaiming the Gospel he brought from his Father (Matt. 4:1–16).

At the first stage of his Proclamation journey, Jesus preaches two tiny homilies in few words. Among the crowd of Galileans, he preached, "Repent, for the kingdom of heaven is at hand" (Matt. 4: 17); and at the Sea of Galilee, he did preach to his first disciples, "Come after me, and I will make you fishers of men" (Matt. 4:18–22). Jesus, according to Matthew, didn't end up his preaching ministry in that kind of "wordy" way. Rather, while the Master "went around all of Galilee, teaching in their synagogues, proclaiming the gospel of the kingdom, he too was curing every disease and illness among the people" (Matt. 4: 23–25).

Keeping those events as the most leading and aptly validating backdrop to Jesus's longest Sermon on the Mount, Matthew accounts it in three following chapters. As a preface to the Sermon on the Mount, the writer fittingly places, as a preface, a list of Jesus's wishes and dreams about the new Life, which his followers would be possessing by walking through his Way of Truth.

If we deeply meditate all that Matthew covers in the Sermon on the Mount, we will learn that Jesus is directing us to be perfect as God is perfect; and in order to uphold such divine perfection, he has recommended and even ordered us to do many virtuous acts, which can be categorized very succinctly under three headings: Justice, Mercy, and Fidelity. They can be discussed and explained separately but have to be linked together in applying them. Each virtue cannot find its full meaning without the other two.

Besides the eight beatitudes, there is a tenth beatitude that Jesus exposed when he was bringing home to us about our final judgment. The hallmark of this beatitude is that it comes straight out of the Father while all other beatitudes are uttered by his mouth: "Come, you who are blessed by my Father. Inherit the kingdom prepared for you from the foundation of the world. For I was hungry and you gave me food, I was thirsty and you gave me drink, a stranger and you welcomed me, naked and you clothed me, ill and you cared for me, in prison and you visited me" (Matt. 25:34–36). The Heavenly Father showers a special beatitude exclusively to those who do not merely talk or meditate and pray about, but who also perform the works of his mercy to the needy. "If the church does not assume the sentiments of Jesus, it is disoriented, it loses its sense. The beatitudes, in the end, are the mirror in which we see ourselves, that which permits us to know if we are walking on the right path: it is a mirror that does not lie," thus Pope Francis exhorted the participants of the decennial conference of Italian church at Florence (NCR 11-10-15).

That is what Jesus intended. Divine perfection is encountered in this way, and therefore, in order for us to be perfect as God is, we must be simultaneously just, merciful, and faithful. The Bible, inspired by God's Spirit, amazingly selected a Hebrew word that can spell out this "three in one divinely integrated perfection," namely, CHESED. On this backdrop, every Christian, the committed disciple of Jesus, is supposed to practice a Godly Mercy, which is indeed the CHESED-oriented Mercy. Since I discovered the term *mercy* and its prefixed adjectives being handled in multifarious ways by translators, I call, through my lengthy discussions in this book, my readers' attention to its original reading because it seems to me not only to mean mercy but also much more.

This book bases all its content on this phenomenal term as it proceeds to explicate the divine virtues of Justice, Mercy, and Fidelity. Beginning with explaining clearly the deepest meaning of CHESED and going through how CHESED is found in God, in Jesus, and in the Church, the book will complete its purpose by listing out the ways and means we as individuals can perfectly put CHESED into our lives as Jesus expects. As is customary, I will treat the content in details scripturally, traditionally, and surely with my personal experiences.

We are blessed by celebrating the Holy Year of Mercy, as declared by Pope Francis, from December 8, 2015, to November 20, 2016. Exhorting us to perform certain religious and spiritual practices throughout this holy year, the pope emphasized that the main goal of all those performances is to animate every Christian's life by imbibing and spreading the Gospel of mercy. We are also advised to live this year in the light of the Lord's words: "Be merciful, just as your Father is merciful" (Luke 6: 36). Certainly, this jubilee journey starts with a spiritual conversion, proceeds in contemplation and action, and not just end with close adherence to love command of Jesus but to be continued till our last breath.

The entire world hears the Catholic church bells ringing loudly and clearly that her members are making strides slowly but firmly in achieving a renewal by God's mercy, already demonstrated and bestowed in the death and resurrection of Jesus. The end result will be that every church member becoming an agent of divine mercy, as Pope Francis spelled out, a channel through which God can water the earth, protect all its life and matter and make justice and peace flourish.

Enlisting the events designed for celebrating the Jubilee Year of Mercy, Archbishop Salvatore Fisichella, president of the Pontifical Council for Promoting the New Evangelization, said that the Door of Mercy will be opened in local dioceses on the first day of the Year, symbolizing the specialty of the Year in opening the path of mercy for church members and other friends in their strenuous pilgrimage to Eternity by being reawakened to the new evangelization and the pastoral conversion the pope had indicated. He too stressed that this would be an occasion for renewing and rejuvenating all believers who live in a particular way the experience of mercy (5-5-15 Zenith.com).

The church never forgets that this Door of Mercy has been already opened by Jesus for the entire human race. He credited himself as the Gate (John 10:7). He too dreamed that the church he established on the Rock of Peter would be the genuine "gate" to his sheepfold. During the "Holy Journey of Mercy," I want to energize and inspire my Christian brothers and sisters in their desire to attain all the graces from it. Plus, I dream of my readers standing, at their life after death, in front of the

Judge Jesus hearing him joyfully that they were selected to inherit the Ninth Beatitude: "Come, you who are blessed by my Father. Inherit the kingdom prepared for you from the foundation of the world."

The Door of Mercy, as a symbolic ritual sign, can be opened and closed as the Jubilee Year starts and ends. But the Grand Door of eternal Mercy of God is open forever. Perhaps due to the closing of our hearts, we may try to shut the Door of Mercy or we may not be eager to enter through it. Exhibiting his broken heart regarding the post effects of church synods, Cardinal Walter Kasper was quoted as saying, "The synod opened a door, though we did not stride through." The same can be said of the hardheartedness of many church members toward God's clarion call to encounter his mercy, which is not merely pitying but enduring in loving, forgiving, sharing, and sacrificing for the good of the entire human race. Saint Augustine, who was a sinner once but converted by the immense mercy of God, writes about mercy in every human's life: "*Misericordia* (mercy) *and miseria* (misery) *are two sides of the same coin.*" With no exception whatsoever, every human superior or inferior, hierarchy or laity, has to deal with this "double-edged sword" that is hanging over their heads; it is each one's valor and destiny, either to make the best use of it or the worst.

This book is nothing but an outcome of my strong belief in an eternal fact of living a CHESED-oriented life: *Without God's CHESED we cannot survive; but without our CHESED we cannot be what we are designed to become.*

Rev. Benjamin A. Vima

Note to the readers:

My sincere thanks to Zenit.com, Commonweal magazine.com, National Catholic Reporter.com, and Vatican Blog from where all quotes of popes had been taken and used in this book.

I too gratefully acknowledge that all the scriptural verses used here are from the NABRE Bible Translation.

SECTION I

The CHESED Rhizome of Mercy

For Hashem is good; His **chesed** *is l'olam;*
and His **emunah** *endureth dor vador.*
—Psalm 100:5, Orthodox Jewish Bible

Good indeed is the LORD; his **mercy** *endures forever;*
his **faithfulness** *lasts through every generation.*
—Translated in NABRE

In most of our scriptural books, the Hebrew term CHESED is translated as "mercy" or "compassion." According to Rabbi Harold M. Kamsler, a biblical scholar and writer, the English term *mercy* or *compassion* for the translation of this Hebrew word used in the Bible is not correct (Ref. Nelson Glueck, CHESED in the Bible [Cincinnati: Hebrew Union College Press, 1967]). Rabbi Kamsler's contention is that most of those translations use this term to point out only the singular attitude and actions of God; however, in reality, it describes a mutual relationship between man and God. Rabbi Kamsler suggests that the best English word to use as a translation for CHESED would be "loyalty." Though we may agreeably disagree with such statement, as we go deeper into the analysis of this term, we unearth its genuine meaning and its relevance to expound the divine backdrop to the term *mercy*, which we treat in this book.

CHAPTER 1

⊶⊷⊶⊷⊶⊷

The Popular Use of the Term Mercy

The adjective *merciful* refers to somebody or some event that brings someone relief from something unpleasant. It also has as its synonyms: *forgiving, compassionate, clement, pitying, forbearing, lenient, humane, mild, kind, softhearted, tenderhearted, gracious, sympathetic, humanitarian, liberal, tolerant, indulgent, generous, magnanimous, benign, benevolent,* and more.

First of all, we should know that the term *mercy* is a freelance usage of the French word *merci* from 1066, referring to the spirit and action of compassion or forgiveness shown toward someone whom it is within one's power to punish or harm. When we apply it to God with the light of scriptures and Christian tradition, we name it *grace* to denote the fact that God is blessing us despite the fact that we do not deserve it. Mercy is deliverance from judgment. Grace is extending kindness to the unworthy. And when God is not punishing us as our sins deserve, we call it "mercy" (Ref. Online Blog 'Got Questions? org).

So many centuries, millions of us have been accustomed to using this term in our private and liturgical prayers. Undoubtedly, the origin of it is our scriptures, which were sharpened and shaped by Christian traditions. From the second century, as Arrian writes in *Diatribæ Epicteti*, II, 7, the Greek Kyrie Eleison, translated in English "Lord have mercy," has been used by Christians in invoking God. This Christian use was based on the scriptural usages of the same, both in OT (for example, Psa. 4:2, 6:3, 9:14, 25:11, 121:3; Isa. 33:2; Tob. 8:10) and NT (Matt. 9:27, 20:30, 15:22; Mark 10:47; Luke 16:24, 17:13).

This formula of prayer or litany most of the time in the liturgies is used by us as a parrot's rattling, not fully grasping its meaning and background. While all the Eastern rites use the form Kyrie Eleison constantly, Roman Catholic rites, especially in the Mass, this is recited or sung before important parts of the Eucharist, for example, at its beginning and before Holy Communion.

Surely the only time most of us recite it from the depths of our soul is when we feel guilty of our sinfulness and when we think of our final hours. And that too many times is handled as a source of getting a cathartic experience to release my emotional disturbances. But as any other strategies offered to us by the Church, the recitation of "Lord have mercy" contains in it some amazing spiritual in-depth treasure that will assist us in attaining our jubilee year goal. To benefit the most out of the application of "mercy" in our life this jubilee year and the years to come, we should first get into mercy's real meaning and its scriptural background.

CHAPTER 2

Viewing Mercy through
Biblical Spectrum

The Hebrew word חֶסֶד, HESED or CHESED used in the Hebrew Bible, is one of the richest, most powerful words in the Old Testament. Our beloved authors of scriptural books, due to their human ability or inability and being enamored of their close encounter with God's HESED, tried their best to explain it by many nouns and verbs available at their times, using allegorical or metaphoric poetic styles to personify the divine activities contained in the Hebrew word *HESED*.

Historically, the Hebrew term CHESED has proved itself a very challenging one to be translated in its full meaning. Biblical scholars have often complained about this difficulty, especially in translating it into English, because it really has no precise equivalent in our language. However, over the years, many tried their best to represent it with all its fullness. English versions usually try to represent it with such words as "loving kindness," "enduring mercy," "steadfast love," "goodness," "favor," "great love without end" and sometimes "faithfulness," "loyalty," but the full meaning of the word cannot be conveyed without an explanation.

As the development of biblical translations in the pursuit of right and relevance, not only to original manuscripts, but also to easier application in particular age and culture, we can see that the original term CHESED has been handled differently both in OT and NT. Just one example: While the OT translation upheld CHESED as covenantal loyalty—"For it is loyalty that I desire, not sacrifice, and knowledge of God rather than burnt offerings" (Hos. 6:6)—in NT, to emphasize the humans' response to the covenant, translators use *mercy* for CHESED "Go and learn the meaning of the words, 'I desire mercy, not sacrifice.' I did not come to call the righteous but sinners" (Matt. 9:13) and "If you knew what this meant, 'I desire mercy, not sacrifice,' you would not have condemned these innocent men" (Matt. 12:7). All these translated words are taken from NABRE.

As the Biblical Translation History testifies, the first translators of the OT (third century BC) in Greek Septuagint version pervasively used the word *ELEOS*, meaning CHESED as "mercy" and "pity." When Christianity was established and spread to the world from the banks of the Thames River in fourth century AD, Jerome, in his Vulgate Latin translation of the entire Bible—OT and NT—used *MISERICORDIA* (mercy) to translate the Greek term ELEOS (ref. to the article by Norman H. Snaith, reproduced from *A Theological Word Book of the Bible*, edited by Alan Richardson (New York: MacMillan, 1951). From those years onward, translators, keeping always the Hebrew CHESED in mind, began coining variety of terms to bring out its deeper meaning.

In most of our scriptural books, *Hesed* is translated as "mercy" or "compassion." According to Rabbi Harold M. Kamsler, a biblical scholar and writer, the English term *mercy* or *compassion* for the translation of the Hebrew word CHESED' used in the Bible is not correct (Ref. Nelson Glueck, *Hesed in the Bible* [Cincinnati: Hebrew Union College Press, 1967]). Rabbi Kamsler's contention is that most of those translations use CHESED' to point out only the singular attitude and actions of God; however, in reality, the Hebrew term CHESED' describes a mutual relationship between man and God. Rabbi Kamsler suggests that the best English word to use as a translation for CHESED' would be "loyalty."

Though we may agreeably disagree with half of such statement, as we go deeper into it, we discover the complete meaning of *hesed*. In the *Brown-Driver-Briggs Hebrew Lexicon* we find that "hesed of man" is described as kindness of men toward men in doing favors and benefits; kindness extended to the lowly, needy, and miserable; mercy, and (rarely) affection or love of Israel to God, piety; lovely appearance. As for the hesed of God, the lexicon notes it denoting God's redemption from enemies and troubles; in preservation of life from death; in quickening of spiritual life; in redemption from sin; in keeping the covenants, with Abraham, with Moses and Israel.

The Hebrew CHESED' is *charis* (grace), as Luther realized when he used the German Gnade for both words. However, agreeing with the rabbi Harold M. Kamsler's findings, some translators of the Bible, particularly the OT books, they have utilized "loyalty" or "faithfulness" to represent CHESED'.

Let us deeply go into some biblical verses where the Hebrew term HESED or CHESED was used and later how the translators have decoded it. For this purpose, I prefer the book of Psalms in OT, mainly because King David was never wearied to repeat in most of his Psalms the presence and importance of God's HESED, which is an embodiment of the virtues of mercy, justice, and faithfulness. Let me quote a few passages where David is overwhelmed with this titillating truth.

Psalm 86

In the Orthodox Jewish Bible, we read in this Psalm many times the term CHESED (HESED), for instance,

For Thou, Adonoi, art tov, and ready to forgive; and plenteous in chesed unto all them that call upon Thee.

The NABRE version translation of the Psalm looks this way:

> Lord, you are good and forgiving, most merciful to all who call on you . . . Your mercy to me is great . . . But you, Lord, are a compassionate and gracious God, slow to anger, abounding in mercy and truth. Turn to me, be gracious to me; give your strength to your servant; save the son of your handmaid.

In the King James Version we find the following:

> For thou, Lord, art good, and ready to forgive; and plenteous in mercy unto all them that call upon thee. For great is thy mercy toward me: and thou hast delivered my soul from the

lowest hell. But thou, O Lord, art a God full of compassion, and gracious, longsuffering, and plenteous in mercy and truth. O turn unto me, and have mercy upon me; give thy strength unto thy servant, and save the son of thine handmaid.

Psalm 143

Psalm 143 contains a prayer of an oppressed person pleading support from God out of his CHESED:

Cause me to hear Thy chesed in the boker . . . And in Thy "CHESED" silence mine enemies, and destroy all them that oppress my nefesh. (Orthodox Jewish Bible)

> In the morning let me hear of your mercy, for in you I trust . . . In your mercy put an end to my foes and all those who are oppressing my soul. (NABRE)

> Let me hear of your steadfast love in the morning . . . In your steadfast love cut off my enemies, and destroy all my adversaries. (NRSV)

Cause me to hear thy lovingkindness in the morning; And of thy mercy cut off mine enemies, and destroy all them that afflict my soul. (King James Version)

Psalm 98:3, 9

In the Orthodox Jewish Bible, we read the following:

> He hath remembered His "CHESED" and
> His emes toward the Bais Yisroel; all the ends
> of ha'aretz have seen the Yeshu'at Eloheinu
> (salvation of our G-d). Before Hashem; for
> He cometh to judge ha'aretz; with tzedek
> shall He judge the tevel, and the people with
> meisharim (uprightness).

NABRE translates the verses in the following manner:

> God has remembered his mercy and
> faithfulness toward the house of Israel . . .
> Before the LORD who comes, who comes to
> govern the earth, to govern the world with
> justice and the peoples with fairness.

In the King James Bible, it is encoded:

> He hath remembered his mercy and his truth
> toward the house of Israel: all the ends of the
> earth have seen the salvation of our God.
> Before the LORD; for he cometh to judge the
> earth: with righteousness shall he judge the
> world, and the people with equity.

Psalm 63: 4(3)

Because Thy "CHESED is better than chayyim.
(Orthodox Jewish Bible)

For your love is better than life. (NABRE)

Because thy lovingkindness is better than life. (King James Version)

> Because your gracious love is better than life itself. (International Standard Version)

> Because experiencing your loyal love is better than life itself. (New English Translation)

Psalm 92:3

We are told that this Psalm is a hymn of praise and thanks for God's faithful deeds. It is usually sung on the Sabbath. In its third verse, while the Hebrew term *Hesed* (Chesed) is preserved in its original form in a Jewish Bible version, all other English-version translators have employed *mercy* and other terms containing a wider meaning of *mercy*:

> To proclaim Thy "CHESED" in the boker, and Thy emunah baleilot. (Orthodox Jewish Bible)

> To show forth thy mercy in the morning and thy faithfulness every night. (Jubilee Bible Version)

> To proclaim your gracious love in the morning and your faithfulness at night (International Standard Version)

To declare your loving kindness in the morning, and your faithfulness every night. (New King James Version)

To proclaim your love at daybreak, your faithfulness in the night. (NABRE and NIV)

Psalm 119:149

This verse is translated in the following ways by many translators:

Hear my voice according unto Thy "CHESED"; Hashem, revive me according to Thy mishpat. (Orthodox Jewish Bible)

Hear my voice in your mercy, O LORD; by your judgment give me life. (NABRE)

In your love hear my voice, O Lord; give me life by your decrees. (Grail)

Hear my voice in your love, O Lord; by your edict give me life. (NAB)

In keeping with Your faithful love, hear my voice. LORD, give me life in keeping with Your justice. (Holman Christian Standard Bible)

Hear my voice according to your gracious love. LORD, revive me in keeping with your justice. (International Standard Version)

Listen to me because of your loyal love! O LORD, revive me, as you typically do! (NET Bible)

In your faithful love, Yahweh, listen to my voice, let your judgements give me life. (New Jerusalem Bible)

Psalm 117:2

This is the shortest of Psalms that invites all people to acknowledge God's supremacy. It sounds like the constant heartbeat of Israelites who vividly understood that their secure existence was indebted entirely to God's condescending fidelity:

For His "CHESED is mighty toward us; and the Emes Hashem endureth l'olam (forever). (Orthodox Jewish Bible)

His mercy for us is strong; the faithfulness of the LORD is forever. (NABRE)

Strong is his love for us; he is faithful forever. (Grail)

The Lord's love for us is strong; the Lord is faithful forever. (NAB)

For his faithful love is strong and his constancy never-ending (New Jerusalem Bible)

For great is his love toward us, and the faithfulness of the Lord endures forever. (Gateway)

For he loves us with unfailing love; the LORD's faithfulness endures forever. (New Living Translation)

For great is his steadfast love toward us, and the faithfulness of the LORD endures forever. (English Standard Version)

For His lovingkindness is great toward us, And the truth of the LORD is everlasting. (New American Standard Version)

For his merciful kindness is great toward us: and the truth of the LORD endureth forever. (King James Bible)

For his loyal love towers over us, and the LORD's faithfulness endures. (NET Bible)

Because his grace has prevailed upon us! Truly, Lord Jehovah is to eternity! (Aramaic Bible in plain English)

His mercy toward us is powerful. The LORD's faithfulness endures forever. (God's Word Translation)

> For His mercy is great toward us; and the
> truth of the LORD endureth forever. (JPS
> Tanakh 1917)

Psalm 63, for instance, is a hymn of David, who composed it according to biblical scholars while he was in the wilderness of Judah. While there are many other Psalms, like Psalm 23, which portray the connections and interactions happening between God and humans, Psalm 63 splendidly expresses the intimate relationship existing between God and his devotees. David seeks his God day and night, with his body yearning and with his soul thirsting as if in a parched, lifeless land. It is because he believes that God is his savior, living joyfully in the shadow of his wings; his soul clings fast to God who mutually upholds him with his right hand.

For our purpose, let us take one verse from this Psalm: "God's love is better than life." It surely demonstrates David's resilient conviction about God's favorable and loving interaction with him. What kind of interaction is he talking about? The Aramaic word *Chasdecha*, found in the original manuscript, has been translated in many interpreted ways. What I am quoting here is "God's love" from my usually used NABRE translation. But if we browse some other translations, we will come to understand the full content of this Spirit-revealed term: "steadfast love" (ESV); "loving kindness" (KJV and ASV); "mercy" (BBE); "faithful love" (CEB); "grace (TCJB); "constant love" (GNT); "loyal love" (LEB). We can derive from all these various translations that the terms *love, mercy, kindness, grace,* and so on are only the exposition of various dimensions of God's CHESED'.

Psalm 100 is a hymn inviting the people to enter the Temple courts with thank offerings for the God who created them. We can observe in this Psalm how the Psalmist has been preoccupied with the HESED of God as he includes it to be in many of his Psalms as this so that God's people cannot but forget the covenantal deal they and God have made when they said "Amen" to his thunderous but sweet voice. We too can see in verse 100:5 how the original Hebrew word HESED (CHESED) has been handled by different translators:

> For Hashem is good; His "CHESED" is l'olam; and His emunah (faithfulness) endureth dor vador. (Orthodox Jewish Bible)

> Good indeed is the LORD, his mercy endures forever, his faithfulness lasts through every generation. (NABRE)

> For the Lord is good; his mercy is everlasting; and his truth endureth to all generations. (King James Version)

> For the Lord is good. His loyal love endures, and he is faithful through all generations. (NET)

> For the Lord is good and his love endures forever; his faithfulness continues through all generations. (New International Translation)

In addition to the two meanings contained in CHESED, if we begin to read many of the biblical verses, adding *loyalty* wherever "CHESED comes, especially the Psalms, we would be amazed to get a deeper insight on "HESED." Let us take for an example Psalm 136 and add the word *loyalty*. We would not only hear the Psalm sounding better, but it would also make more sense to the revelation of God to us:

> Praise the LORD, for he is good; because forever is His loyalty (for his mercy endures forever)
>
> Praise the God of gods; because forever is His loyalty (for his mercy endures forever)
>
> Praise the Lord of lords; because forever is His loyalty (for his mercy endures forever)

When we recite the whole Psalm in this way, we will discover a new turning point in our understanding and appreciating of God's mercy. Jesus did use the Hebrew term CHESED" in all of his sayings. As we did to Psalm verses, if we add the term *loyalty* instead of *mercy*, we will be thrilled to admire at Jesus's sayings on mercy. For example, let us take Matthew 12:1-9, where we come across one of those events of question and answer between him and the Pharisees. It is about the fulfillment of Sabbath laws and regulations. At the end of his answer, he underlines the importance of CHESED', namely, loyalty, quoting a verse from Hosea:

> For it is loyalty that I desire, not sacrifice, and knowledge of God rather than burnt offerings. (Hos. 6: 6)

CHAPTER 3

The Staggering End Result of Proper CHESED Usage

Very interestingly, when we browse the Bible, we are told that this CHESED which belongs solely to God, is shared mutually to humans if they make covenant with God. In the book of Genesis, we read Abraham's servant, who was sent by his master to find a good wife for Isaac, praying to God: "LORD, God of my master Abraham, let it turn out favorably for me today and thus deal graciously with (show 'Hesed' to) my master Abraham" (Gen. 24:12). This means when humans are loyal to their Creator, He too in turn will be loyal to them.

King David was never wearied to repeat in most of his Psalms the presence and importance of God's CHESED, which is an embodiment of the virtues of mercy, justice, and faithfulness. Let me quote a few passages where David is overwhelmed with this titillating truth:

> Lord, you are good and forgiving, most merciful to all who call on you . . . Your mercy to me is great . . . But you, Lord, are

a compassionate and gracious God, slow to
anger, abounding in mercy and truth. Turn to
me, be gracious to me; give your strength to
your servant; save the son of your handmaid.
(Ps. 86:5–15)

God has remembered his mercy and
faithfulness toward the house of Israel . . .
Before the LORD who comes, who comes to
govern the earth, to govern the world with
justice and the peoples with fairness. (Ps.
98:3–9)

Let us look into Psalm 85, which might have
been composed during the early postexilic period,
probably fifth BC, and which seems a national lament
of OT Israelites reminding God of his past CHESED
accomplishments and begging him to continue the same
in their current life. If we gather all the activities of
God listed in this Psalm, we can figure out the in-depth
meaning of God's CHESED'.

It portrays that Israelites undoubtedly knew about
God's CHESED, from their personal and social
relationship with God that he cannot tolerate their sins—
he would get wild; he would be very much displeased; he
is truth therefore he cannot compromise it at any cost; he
is peace therefore he cannot tolerate any hatred, disunity;
this means he loved justice enshrined with truth, holiness,
and wisdom.

At the same time, according to his CHESED, people
were ensured that by his very nature, God would deal with
them in mercy: he would favor them; he would restore
them; he would forgive their sins; he would pardon them;

he would withdraw his wrath from them; ultimately, he would show his mercy granting salvation to them.

The third element in CHESED, God's faithfulness, has been the foundation of his people lamenting and begging before God for a second chance. As a weaning child, they approach him again and again for forgiveness, for renewal, and for more and better salvation of joy and peace. And it was their experience that God never failed in his mercy nor was he exhausted in establishing his justice enshrined with holiness, truth, and love. God has been ever faithful in his mercy and justice. If children find that their parents are unfaithful to them, would they go and beg them repeatedly? The same is true in the personal relationship existing between God and his people. This is the source of all the biblical hymns, canticles, lamentations, prayers such as Psalm 85.

Dr. Robert Stackpole, STD, is director of the John Paul II Institute of Divine Mercy, an Anglican priest who became a Catholic, in his work Divine Mercy, talks about the "semantic problem" existing in the use of the term *mercy* right from the start of the works of translating the Bible. He states that the term *mercy* in contemporary English has a very restricted meaning to refer to like an act of pardon. Catholic theology, traditionally upholding *mercy* in the salvific history of God, signifies more than mere revocation of punishment. Also, Dr. Stackpole's research study on the term *mercy* exposes translators of the Bible who have been using *mercy* to mean two Hebrew words: one, which we extensively discuss in this book, CHESED meaning "steadfast love, covenant love"; and the other *rachamim*, that indicates a person's tender, compassionate love, a love that springs from pity. Dr. Stackpole writes the following: "*According to the Catholic*

Biblical scholar John L. Mckenzie, the word chesed is often used in Hebrew in connection with other words which bring out its meaning, such as chesed-emet (steadfast, dependable love), chesed-sedekah (righteous, holy love) and chesed-yesua (rescuing, saving love)."

He too quotes Blessed Pope John Paul II from the endnote to his encyclical *Dives in misericordia* (Rich in mercy) through which we can grasp the pope's understanding of the amazing meaning of the term :

When in the Old Testament the word chesed is used of the Lord, this always occurs in connection with the covenant that God established with Israel. This covenant was, on God's part, a gift and a grace for Israel . . . God had made a commitment to respect it . . . [this divine chesed] showed itself as what it was at the beginning, that is, as a love that gives, love more powerful than betrayal, grace stronger than sin. (no. 52)

The Catholic Bible scholar John L. Mckenzie says in the *Dictionary of the Bible*:

The entire history of the dealing of Yahweh with Israel can be summed up as chesed; it is the dominating motive which appears in his deeds, and the motive which gives unity and intelligibility to all His dealings with men.

Being a mystic and lovable humane being, Blessed Pope John Paul shared his enriching meditative thought on the word *mercy* and how its Hebrew roots and rachamim fall in line with our celebration of the Divine Mercy. In his *Dives in misericordia*, he connects both together to portray God's mercy. The blessed pope considers CHESED as, in a way, a masculine form of love that is always steadfast, dependable, righteous, being true to oneself and to one's promises, whereas RACHAMIM is more feminine, denoting God's mercy like that of a tender, responsive, and compassionate mother responding in love to her suffering child.

In biblical theology, we come across great emphasis on the God-and-humans covenantal aspect of hesed, which stands more than any other word for the attitude that both parties to a covenant ought to maintain toward each other. We discover in the Scriptures brightly that the attitude and behavior of the almighty, just, and merciful God are founded on the covenant, both old and new, which he had made with his chosen ones. Moreover, we notice that all religious, social, and spiritual commands; orders; rubrics; practices; and rituals God had promulgated through his messengers, especially Moses and Jesus, are for his chosen ones to respond to their divine partner as reciprocal covenantal commitments and observances. Thus, the deeper the study on this covenantal relationship existing between God and his people for which the Hebrew term CHESED had been always used, the clearer its in-depth meaning becomes.

First of all, we should understand how the covenant word CHESED, especially of the treaty made between God and his people, was widened in its meaning. According to the experience and inspiration of the sacred authors, there is no guile or deviation or unfaithfulness on the part of God as the main party in the covenant; but they noticed a continual waywardness of the second party, the Israel, in reciprocating God's covenant. Despite their unfaithfulness and dishonesty, the same authors discovered that God never let his people go that whimsical way of perdition and they too were of one mind to confirm the necessity of the enduring mercy in God. Consequently, they began stressing more on God's forgiveness, loving kindness, graciousness, and goodness for which certainly the people were undeserving of. Due to such pathetic and pitiable status of the people's reciprocal response to covenant, it was very clear to the sacred authors that God's mercy should be in immense, eccentric, and unfathomable standard. That is how mercy, one of the three elements that are prescribed in the term HESED, became the main core of thrust in most of the sacred writings.

Enlightened by biblical authors, scholars, and church fathers, we can perceive the full meaning of the Hebrew term CHESED, as a tripod of mercy, justice, and faithfulness, which should be fully attributed to God; but the same also can be possessed by humans in a limited way and by the grace of God. The latter can be contended by the revelation from the book of Genesis that humans are created in the image and likeness of God; secondly, we too can arrive at this conclusion from the other books of the Bible where we can observe that God's love for his humans mutually demonstrate this hesed. He too commands us to be just, to be merciful, and to be as faithful as he is to us. Mercy therefore cannot be treated as an isolated virtue. It gets its full identity only when it is esteemed as 'CHESED' consisting of justice, mercy and faithfulness.

From all that have been said in this section, the term *merciful*, used here in this book or by any church member, cannot ignore its beautiful and meaningful scriptural and revelatory background of CHESED which more fittingly can be explained in the following way:

God is faithfully just and merciful.

God is faithfully just in his holiness and truth.

God is faithfully merciful in his justice and peace.

God is uncompromisingly faithful in his justice.

God is relentlessly faithful in his mercy.

SECTION II

∗∙❖▦▬▬▬▬▬❖▬▬▬▬▬▦❖∙∗

The Mercy of Just and Faithful God

*Hashem is rachum and channun, slow to
anger, and plenteous in chesed.*

—Psalm 103:8, OJB

*Merciful and gracious is the LORD, slow
to anger, abounding in mercy.*

—Psalm 103:8, NABRE

I love to say that our God is "Three-in-One." I am not
referring here to the dogma of Trinity. Rather, in this
section, I want to throw some light on another triple
dimension of our God spelled out throughout the Bible,
which, using the amazing term CHESED (HESED),
reiterates that the Almighty is synchronously just and
merciful and faithful.

CHAPTER 4

•◦•❖•▓▒░▬▬▬▬▬▬▬▬▬▬◆▬▬▬▬▬▬▬▬▬░▒▓•❖•◦•

God's CHESED Project

The Good Book is filled with expositions of who God is and how he lives and interacts with humans. There are many attributes to his personality, among which the most striking and liking to our hearts are that he is just and he also is merciful. The Bible is filled with many adjectives to qualify God, such as just, merciful, wise, infinite, sovereign, holy, triune, all-knowing, faithful, loving, all-powerful, self-existing, self-sufficient, immutable, eternal, good, gracious, righteous, and omnipresent.

All other ideas about God as found in other religions and even among our Christian writers and preachers are, according to the Bible, false gods. They are from the imagination of mankind. However, we can never deny the fact that most of the non-Christian religious scriptures declare that God is both loving and merciful. For our discussion in this book, we have taken three main attributes to God, namely, mercy, justice, and fidelity. We should remember, here as we treat these attributes of God, how all the translators encountered continuous struggle in translating the Hebrew term CHESED and how staggeringly these three attributes evenly and unmistakably pervaded throughout the Bible.

Regarding this three-in-one nature of God, let me share here just two illustrations from the OT. In a hymn of praise (chapter 13), Tobit repeats like a litany how he and his people held reverentially God's CHESED in its triple dimensions. While God out of his righteousness (God's quality or state of being just or rightful) afflicts and casts sinful humans down to the bottomless pit (Hades), he too shows his bottomless mercy. Psalm 33 is another hymn of praise to God who is testified as upright in his word, as trustworthy in his works, as a lover of justice and right. The earth is full of his mercy, his plans stand forever through all generations, he delivers from perils and life problems all those who count on his mercy.

If we study deeply all the biblical references about the attributes of God, we can contend that all of them can be listed under three categories of justice and mercy and fidelity. While almost all carry *all* or *ever* or *omni* as their prefixes, to denote the fidelity of the Divine, the attributes of wisdom, infinitude, sovereignty, holiness, omniscience, omnipotence, self-existence, self-sufficiency, immutability, eternity, and omniscience can fall under the category of God's justice; and all other attributes can be listed under God's mercy. God seems, because of his faithful nature, to never stop being merciful to us unless we choose to despise or ignore God at which time his justice, the other dimension of his personality, becomes the prominent activator in his divine administration.

Human nature is always leaning more on justice than mercy, and that too only against others, and not oneself. More than ever before, today we are inclined to be a generation of "getting even" and "feeling happy" with others. We forget the true existence and meaning of mercy. Many of us have developed a nature of harshly criticizing others' conduct and judging expeditiously, as if sitting on the throne of Moses, that they should get punished for what they deserve. On the contrary, God is merciful to even the worst offenders, sinners, and law breakers. His mercy is not just to avoid all offensive deeds against them but also continue to shower his blessings for their survival as he does to his goodwilled children. He is kind to the ungrateful and the wicked (Luke 6:35b; Matt. 5:45).

A preacher told a story to expound the immense and indescribable quality of God's mercy. The story was about a mother who once approached Napoleon asking for a pardon for her son. Napoleon replied that the young man had twice committed a certain crime and that for justice to be done, the man deserved to die. "But I don't ask for justice," the mother explained. "I plead for mercy."

"But your son does not deserve mercy," replied Napoleon.

"It would not be mercy if he deserved it, and mercy is all that I seek for him," replied the mother.

Because of the mother's sound and clear reasoning, Napoleon said, "Well then, I will have mercy," and he spared the woman's son. That is how God's mercy is: It is a gift given to those who don't deserve it.

In a very outstanding way, Jesus proclaimed this three-in-one identity of God. He did this through a tiny parable of the fig tree (Luke 13:6–9). The fig tree represents the fruitless inability of sinful humans, and the two persons, who are debating with each other about the fate of the fig tree, symbolize vividly the two virtues of God: the owner of the orchard who epitomizes the justice side of

God and the gardener who personifies his second side of being compassionate and enduring patience (faithfulness). Ultimately, the winner is the compassionate identity of God, who is eternally patient with his humans, waiting and waiting, in their pathway of life for their conversion from sinfulness. The fidelity of the merciful and just God is patient and gives everyone a chance.

At the same time, Jesus never missed to remind his contemporaries the just side of God's nature by explaining the historical accidents and calamities that occurred at his time as well as in biblical history (Luke 13:1-5). As matter of fact, Jesus insists on how God's compassion and mercy can wear out because he is just and he will punish the sinners.

Though Gospel writers list many conditions to follow Jesus as his disciples, they underscore the effective strategy of maintaining our discipleship with Jesus in order to claim our rewards from God, which is nothing but a twofold action: "To be just as the heavenly Father is just" and "To be merciful as the Almighty is merciful." There is no alternate way to attain the heavenly crown for all that we accomplish as Jesus's disciples. In this regard, Paul is our role model.

Disciples of Jesus preached the same strategy for salvation to adhere to the threefold strategy Jesus endorsed. In their messages, they presented God's double intertwined virtues: his resolute justice and his enduring mercy. Paul, in his letter (1 Cor. 10:1-12), points out how God could not tolerate the disobedience and indifference of human beings, especially his chosen ones. He writes that our merciful God, though he did so many miraculous deeds for the life, freedom, and happiness of his people, was not pleased with most of them and therefore struck them down in the desert; he even destroyed them all because of their evil deeds. God thus showed his nature of being just. At the same time, Paul also adds that the same God, out of compassion, had led his people through the saving waters and given them manna to eat despite that many failed to respond to his love and perished.

As a holy and heavenly Father, God's only dream is that all of his human children should attain their destiny. An entire lifetime is given to each one of us to bear fruits to carry with us to the eternal life. At the same time, God knows that we, on our way to eternity, fail, stumble, fall, faint, detour, deviate due to our human weakness, sinfulness, ignorance, perverted freedom, and pride. With deep concern for us, God waits for our complete winning.

In compassion, he is patiently in his fidelity waiting for our conversion and sanctification. He gives us freedom to choose to rise up and to return to him; he too gives a long rope and allows us to prolong our indifference, coldness, and carelessness and even permits us to go to hit the bottom. It is left to us either to catch the same rope and climb up from the pit or to use the same rope to hang and ruin ourselves. He uses the signs of the time to bring us back to our right senses and to view our life as it is. These signs are those natural calamities, disasters happening around us, other people's sickness, death, and especially all the evil things that occur to us in our private and family life. God waits for our conversion. This is God's justice-oriented compassion.

Jesus underlines the uniqueness of God's faithful behavior toward his creatures as a just but merciful Proprietor. In his parable of the workers in the vineyard, he deliberates this truth. The landowner of a vineyard who symbolizes God, the Landowner of the universe, hires workers at different hours of the day. Very surprisingly, at the end of the day, he handed out wages to the workers the same amount of money to everyone with no distinction. While the workers who started their work very early at daybreak saw the owner giving to those who joined them as late as 5:00 p.m. the same amount of wages they were given, certainly, they were indignant with the unjust behavior of their hirer. But the landowner retorted to them: "My friend, I am not cheating you. Did you not agree with me for the usual daily wage? Take what is yours and go. What if I wish to give this last one the same as you? Or am I not free to do as I wish with my own money? Are you envious because I am generous?"

This is how our God is. He demonstrates his justice in mercy. We should know that God possesses all right on us, especially in the "hire and fire" in choosing and rewarding in his kingdom. However, by this action, as narrated by Jesus, God seems judging and rewarding humans not by what they accomplish but by how needy and how worthy they are in his sight. Fidelity, compassion, and justice are amazingly intertwined in the Creator.

CHAPTER 5

The Immense Mercy of the Just and Faithful God

The Uniqueness in the Tender Mercy of God

> Because of the tender mercy of our God by
> which the daybreak from on high will visit
> us to shine on those who sit in darkness and
> death's shadow, to guide our feet into the
> path of peace. (Luke 1:78-79)

I was startled to read a description about God's love
and mercy, pointed out in this Gospel passage in
a traditional devotional hymn. The composer sings,
"His heart is made of tenderness, his bowels melt with
love." Explaining this lyric in his own poetical but very
inspirational style, Reverend Spurgeon said in one of
his sermons: "'Mercy' is music, and 'tender mercy' is the
most exquisite form of it, especially to a broken heart."
Besides, when I caught sight of some more sermons and
writings of preachers and saints on the scriptural portrays
of God's "tender mercy," I was so much delighted that I

intensely studied about it and came out with some striking conclusions on the mercy of God toward humans.

Those were the prophetic words sung by Zachariah, the father of John the Baptizer, in his canticle of praise to the Creator for the divine intervention in his son's birth. He stressed the most revealing fact of God's redemptive action in and through Jesus Christ out of his tender mercy. What I am quoting here is from the NABRE translation. I was curious to know the in-depth meaning of the adjective *tender* added to *mercy*. I browsed many different translations of this verse. I came out with different translations, such as "bottomless," "tender mercy of God," "mercy of the bowels," or "of the inwards," or "of his heart" and son.

In misinterpreting these terms, some consider God's mercy as very emotional. They are totally wrong. Witnessing a pathetic and horrible news on television about crying, bleeding, and starving kids, most of us would shed some tears and want to help. This does not necessarily mean that we are merciful. Undoubtedly, those who are merciful will often experience deep emotions, but just because a person is emotional doesn't make them merciful. Only we humans are good enough to fake being merciful through some outward emotionalism. Even some of us may do good things to the needy through which we may be judged by the public as merciful persons; on the contrary, those mercy acts would have performed for selfish reasons.

God's mercy is not at all to be considered that way. All those terms used in many linguistic translations for mercy of God indicate only its in-depth and intensive characteristic. Mercy is his nature, his drive, and his powerful Self. Mercy in the Bible is the attribute of God, which disposes Him to be actively compassionate. It will never end since it is a part of God's nature. Mercy is the way he likes to relate to humans. In the OT, we find numerous references on this truth:

> Who is a God like you, who removes guilt and pardons sin for the remnant of his inheritance; who does not persist in anger forever, but instead delights in mercy? (Mic. 7:18)

> God's mercy can make even the driest land become a garden, can restore life to dry bones. (Cf. Ezra 37:1–14)

> Come now, let us set things right, says the LORD: Though your sins be like scarlet, they may become white as snow; though they be red like crimson, they may become white as wool. (Isa. 1:18)

> Good indeed is the LORD, His mercy endures forever; his faithfulness lasts through every generation. (Ps. 100:5)

The true God whom we worship is a God of love, compassion, forgiveness, goodness, justice, and peace. He is a God of life. Bundling all those characteristics into one package, we can say in the biblical Hebrew word *HESED*, meaning "His Loyalty." God's loyalty in mercy cannot be conditioned; it always goes ahead of us. As the Scriptures underlines, His Spirit (mercy) blows where it wills. In this regard, Saint Thomas says that in God, mercy is the highest virtue and forgiveness is the highest manifestation of the divine power. The forgiveness that Jesus won for us on the cross had no condition.

The Unthinkable Merciful Deeds of a Just God

Asking us not to forget God's marvelous gifts to us, David describes about those magnificent gifts:

The LORD does righteous deeds, brings justice to all the oppressed. He made known his ways to Moses, to the Israelites his deeds. Merciful and gracious is the LORD, slow to anger, abounding in mercy (CHESED). (Ps. 103:6–8)

He pardons all our sins; heals all our ills; redeems our life from the pit; crowns us with mercy and compassion; fills our days with good things so our youth is renewed like the eagle's, which is the biblical symbol of perennial youth and vigor; brings justice to all the oppressed; doesn't always accuse us; nurses no lasting anger; does not deal with us as our sins merit nor requites us as our wrongs deserve. His mercy towers over those who fear him like the heavens; as far as the east is from the west, so far will he remove our sins from us; as a father has compassion on his children, so he has compassion on those who fear him; this is all because he knows sufficiently well our vulnerable and fragile human life.

"God, who is rich in mercy, because of the great love he had for us, even when we were dead in our transgressions, brought us to life with Christ by grace you have been saved" (Eph. 2:4–5). There are some among us as those in Paul's time who mistakenly think that God is a God of mercy and grace, so we can just keep sinning and be forgiven and live like we want. We can understand this. Fragile people as we are, it is hard for us first to understand, then to grasp and uphold God's HESED; and worse, our human weakness cannot mutually reciprocate it to the Almighty. Paul had a clear picture of this human truth: "I urge you therefore, brothers, by the mercies of God, to offer your bodies as a living sacrifice, holy and pleasing to God, your spiritual worship" (Rom. 12:1). What we read here is a specimen of Paul's own style of beginning his exhortations. A man who had his second life by the mercy of God and who encountered the same divine mercy in many life situations naturally would have been overwhelmed with the HESED of God in Jesus. Plus, he would have felt that without the same HESED, his Christian readers and listeners to his messages would in no way comprehend and follow what he was preaching. That is why he started every one of his exhortation underlining the mercies of God.

Nonetheless, Paul ruthlessly criticized them, writing: "What then shall we say? Shall we persist in sin that grace may abound? Of course not! How can we who died to sin yet live in it?" (Rom. 6:1–2). All reasonable persons agree with the Apostle that God did not pour out his mercy so we could sin more, knowing that we don't have to pay the consequences. God is not a goody-goody grandpa who cares only about the pleasure of his grandchild at a particular moment. But he is very attentive to our entire life and its grand goal of eternity even though countless times he does forgive our evil doings.

God Is Exceptional in His Ways

> Thus says the LORD to his anointed, Cyrus, whose right hand I grasp, subduing nations before him, stripping kings of their strength, opening doors before him, leaving the gates unbarred . . . For the sake of Jacob, my

> servant, of Israel my chosen one, I have called
> you by name, giving you a title, though you do
> not know me . . . It is I who arm you, though
> you do not know me . . . so that all may know,
> from the rising of the sun to its setting, that
> there is none besides me. I am the LORD,
> there is no other. (Isa. 45:1-6)

> Thus says the LORD, the Holy One of Israel,
> his maker: Do you question me about my
> children, tell me how to treat the work of my
> hands? (Isa. 45:11)

God's mercy, on the face of it, may appear to humans
as very illogical and eccentric. The scriptural idea of
God's mercy includes the emotionality of God along
with His spiritual nature. We encounter a biblical God
who has deep emotions and who feels delight, anger, and
frustration. He compares his feelings as those of pregnant
mothers at their pangs in the delivery of their babies. We
too notice him being affected by his humans. Despite the
warnings of God about his awe-inspiring holy Presence,
when his holy messengers, like Abraham, Moses, Isaiah,
David and others, demonstrated their loyalty to His
HESED, he permitted himself to be very familiar to them
as a friend, lover, and companion. In other words, his
mercy made him a typical person in its right meaning.
His one only preoccupation and longing was to be loved
by them. I tend to join with C. S. Lewis who is quoted in
the book *Sealed Orders* by Agnes Sanford: "God is always
saving people in ways I don't like."

Jesus's parable of the prodigal son (Luke 15:11-32)
is also aptly called the story of the prodigal father. The

term *prodigal* is defined as "spendthrift," "wasteful," "reckless," "extravagant," and "uncontrolled." We discover the same kind of father in the parable through which Jesus illustrates very lucidly the unique and incredible mercy-driven behavior of God; he may seem like reckless, wasteful, spendthrift in showing mercy.

First, as soon as the younger son said to his father, "Give me my share of the estate," the father divided his property between them. He did nothing to prevent his son and did not make any attempt to make him realize that the choice he was making was horrible. Does it not look weird?

Secondly, the younger son left the house or the hometown only after some days. This means the son was still there in front of his father a few days in which the father never did anything to stop him. Doesn't he act strangely?

Thirdly, according to the story, the younger son gathered all his belongings and started off for a distant land where he squandered his wealth in loose living. Having spent everything, he was hard-pressed when a severe famine broke out in that land. So he hired himself out to a well-to-do citizen of that place and was sent to work on a pig farm. So famished was he that he longed to fill his stomach even with the food given to the pigs, but no one offered him anything. Where was that father's concern and love? He should have taken some time to go in search of him or at least sent some of his servants to look for his beloved son. Nothing he did. Doesn't it seem odd?

Fourthly, when the prodigal son returned of his own accord realizing his mistakes, as he was still a long way off, the father caught sight of him. Then the father was so deeply moved with compassion that he ran out to meet him, threw his arms around his neck, and kissed him and gave all royal welcome and unforgettable treat. Does the father not appear reckless?

Finally, there is another peculiar action of this prodigal father. While he did not do anything when his younger son behaved badly, he reacted when his elder son misbehaved in getting angry about his dad's unorthodox behavior. His father came out immediately and exhorted him with a stern advice about his benevolence toward him.

Now the legitimate question arises: Why did Jesus make these anomalous references to God and his mercy? Why did he make Him behave this way, so cold and unconcerned? Is God's fatherly love only a hypocritical lie?

The sincere answer to this question is nothing but Jesus's emphasis on the unfathomable lavishing mercy of God, plus, his desire to make us understand clearly the concept of God's mercy, which is a rare blend of both love and justice. The latter truth can be drawn from comparing Jesus's three parables on the same matter of "lost and found" process of God's mercy (Luke 15:1–32).

In the parables of the lost-and-found coin and the lost-and-found sheep, we hear about coins, which are materials that do not have any life, and about the sheep having life but no free thinking, rationality, freedom, and independence. But the lost-and-found prodigal son is a human being possessing like God a full freedom and independence. With his reason, he has the capacity to make choices for his life.

Let me share my life's fieldwork of making choices, a stage when I was directed and taught by my parents and elders on how to make choices and on what to choose as the best for my life. "Until you are under my umbrella or roof," they said, "you have to abide or obey certain rules and customs prescribed by me." The second stage of my life with God came when I began to think, reason out, and ask questions on anything and everything. I was excited during this period to make my own choices whether they are good or bad, right or wrong. I got angry if I was not permitted to choose my own. I confess that at this stage, I made blunders through my wrong choices as the prodigal son. At the third stage of my life as a grown-up person, with many scars and stains, I began to be melted. I felt sorry about my wrong choices; sometimes planning to redo the whole thing or other times using the past as my learning process, I corrected myself and attempted to do better.

I am positive that almost all of us would have gone through these stages. I think that at this third stage, God would have entered to rescue and redeem us. The word of God points out that our merciful God hugs us when we approach him at this stage. He is too happy to remember what happened in our past. Paul confesses of this merciful gesture of God in his life: I was once a blasphemer and a persecutor and an arrogant man, but I have been mercifully treated because I acted out of ignorance in my unbelief (1 Tim. 1:13).

Scripturally, there are two sides to human life. On one side, life is full of blessings while the other side is full of curses. Human beings must choose of their own accord one of those two. God is the creator of that freedom. He is eternally just and respects his humans' dignity. Certainly God has been, throughout our life's stages, as shown in the Bible, angry and anxious about us and our behavior.

He reveals this justice-oriented attitude to his messengers like Moses.

> Go down at once because your people, whom you brought out of the land of Egypt, have acted corruptly. They have quickly turned aside from the way I commanded them, making for themselves a molten calf and bowing down to it . . . I have seen this people, how stiff-necked they are . . . Let me alone, then, that my anger may burn against them to consume them. (Exod. 32: 7–10)

We Are Shamefully Weird and Not God

I want to highlight one thing here about God's just but merciful relationship with us who are in reality shamefully weird. God is all-powerful. He can touch the stone or desert soil and water can be generated; he can touch the sea and it will divide and he can offer a path to cross it; he can touch clay and man would be created; he can touch the bone and it will turn out to be woman; he can even tough the dead body and it will resurrect. But even if he touches warmly or forcefully any human being, it needs a double miracle for us to do the right thing on God's behalf. We are capable of saying to him, "Stop. First knock at my door, stand there waiting for me until I open it for you. Then you enter into my abode. You have no authorization until I say welcome."

We did not tie his legs or hands to come and stop us from doing evils. Rather, he imprisons himself by his love and respect for us. If he does anything otherwise, he would act against his own nature. So he waits and waits for human beings to return. He can never violate his own holiness and justice. He loves to see them make right choices with their own free will. And that is how as Prodigal Father, as Jesus underscored, God behaves in every human's life.

Mercy of God is sometimes signified in the scriptures as a bottomless abyss in him. It certainly bestows the in-depth nature of his mercy. The entire human race was born in the bottomless pit and is unable to climb out of the bottomless pit by their own strength because it is a bottomless pit. It is a pit without walls and with an infinite depth, out of which no one can climb, not even Satan. But God, who is rich in mercy, even when we were dead in trespasses and sins, has made us alive to Him even while we are living in the midst of death around us here in the bottomless pit. And it is here in the bottomless pit where we are called to serve God by letting our light so shine before men, in the darkness of the bottomless pit, that men may see our good work and glorify our Father who is in heaven. Here in the pitch-dark blackness of this kingdom of Satan we must function as little lights here and there and in this way be the soldiers of Christ who will rob the house of Satan.

John Wesley very poetically and clearly wrote in one of his hymns about the deep meaning of God's bottomless abyss. He listed out God's unfathomable attributes, such as all perfection, unequal greatness, immutability, omnipotence, and immeasurable wisdom (ref. to The Voice of Praise: a collection of hymns for the use of the Methodist Church #48).

The Bible uses the adjective *bottomless* in two cases: in explaining God's unfathomable and immeasurable mercy (Luke 1:78) and in explaining the humans' pitiable state of living in unimaginable depth of sinfulness and darkness (Rev. 9:1). Here, it is all about the hellish milieu of fallen angels who were thrust into that bottomless pit of darkness and fire. When humans unluckily had fallen into that pit by their hardheartedness, hardheadedness, and surely many times because of their imprudence and ignorance, God, out of his bottomless mercy, raises them from that pit by the salvific hands of Jesus. Jesus told Saint Faustina in one of her visions of the Divine Mercy, "Know, my daughter that between me and you there is a bottomless abyss, an abyss which separates the Creator from the creature. But this abyss is filled with my mercy" (Saint Faustina, Divine Mercy in my Soul).

Now we can see why even God knows that we will commit sin and he cannot stop us. Sin promises us a life of momentary pleasure and excitement, but the end of it all is misery, depression, dissatisfaction, and loss of dignity as God's children. There is no use in blaming God if we carelessly waste the blessings he showers upon us. There is no use in blaming God if we destroy our God-given health with harmful habits. Far from God, we acquire the tendency to do evil and neglect our responsibility as parents and children. The good news about this parable is that no matter how deeply we sink into sin, there is always our inner voice that invites us to the Father's house where true freedom and dignity is found.

CHAPTER 6

·•※◈▓▓▬▬▬▬▬▬▬▬◈▬▬▬▬▬▬▬▬▓▓◈※•·

The Incompatible Justice of a Merciful and Faithful God

His Actions Are Right and Fair

When the Bible says "God is just," it underlines God's character that defines what being just really is. He does not conform to some outside criteria. Being just brings moral equity to everyone. We are told he is the ruler, proprietor, and ultimate judge to us. In connection to this fact, the acceptance of the reign of God and righteousness is the grace of God resulting from the acceptance of God's reign. Here are a few verses from Isaiah:

> Let justice descend, you heavens, like dew from above, like gentle rain let the clouds drop it down. Let the earth open and salvation bud forth; let righteousness spring up with them! (Isa. 45:8)
> I, the LORD, promise justice, I declare what is right. (Isa. 45:19b)

> Was it not I, the LORD, besides whom there
> is no other God? There is no just and saving
> God but me. (Isa. 45:21)
>
> By myself I swear, uttering my just decree, a
> word that will not return: To me every knee
> shall bend; by me every tongue shall swear,
> saying, "Only in the LORD are just deeds and
> power. (Isa. 45:23–24)

The Hebrew term *sedeq*, used in the Orthodox Jewish
Bible, is very elusive as many other terms in that language,
referring to or alluding to a variety of God's attributes
such as justice, righteousness, holiness, or goodness. In
most of the passages of the Old Testament and the New
Testament, the words *just* and *righteous* are identical. As
one scholar points out, sometimes the translators render
the original word *just* and other times *righteous* with
no apparent reason. While the writers largely use the
particular term *sedeq* to mean "saving victory" of God
(Isa. 45), we too notice they refer it to "straight," "equal,"
or "right." By writing "God is just," they mean that he
always does what is right, what should be done, and that
he accomplishes it consistently, plus with no partiality or
prejudice whatsoever. For instance, Nehemiah confesses to
the Lord that "he is just because he fulfilled his promises
to his ancestors." He too ascertains that with all the evils
that came upon his people, the Lord had been just; while
people have done evil, God kept faith" (Neh. 9). Basically,
whatever term these writers use, it refers to one thing:
God's actions are always right and fair.

Clarifying the justice of God in his actions, A. W.
Tozer writes in his book *The Knowledge of the Holy*:

> Justice, when used of God, is a name we give
> to the way God is, nothing more; and when
> God acts justly He is not doing so to conform
> to an independent criterion, but simply acting
> like Himself in a given situation. . . God is
> His own self-existent principle of moral
> equity, and when He sentences evil men
> or rewards the righteous, He simply acts
> like Himself from within, uninfluenced by
> anything that is not Himself.

Our Mistaken Views of God's Deeds

Some mistakenly think that the terms *mercy* and *justice* (righteousness) are diametrically opposed. Both are concomitantly the singular nature of God. As Tozer indicates, God simply acts like himself mercifully and justly. When we hear in the Bible that he revealed his righteousness, we should understand that he disclosed his will and his word; he, as a Teacher, instructed humans in his word; he judged the enemies of Israel; shockingly he too judged his chosen ones for their sin and disobedience; he defined the scheme and strategy of his ruling power; he testified to his holiness his hurt feeling, his abhorring against the abominable infidelity of his chosen ones and their wickedness; he exhibited his compassionate heart to protect the poor and the afflicted; he proved his faithful mercy in saving sinners.

In this revealed light, we must first delete from our mind the wrong perception that God's righteousness is revealed in his judgment of sinners and his mercy by his salvation of sinners; secondly we should be convinced of the amazing truth found in God; namely, God's righteousness is the cause of both condemnation and justification. He is righteous in saving sinners, as well as merciful and compassionate.

At this juncture, a small discussion is warranted on the behavior of our just, merciful, and faithful God in his covenantal dealings with humans. It is an uninterrupted human history that while on one side humans out of their weakness slap in the face of a loving God, he on the other side out of his merciful, just, and faithful nature (CHESED) continues to reach out to them, trying to liberate them from all the evil repercussions of sin. A relevant story in OT offers us on this matter. Since the chosen people, ignoring the marvelous deeds of God's loving kindness, living careless about his laws and teachings, were reaping the bad consequences of their blunders, God came again to their rescue. God's love was far-reaching.

In the book of Isaiah (chapter 45), we read God's promise that he would be saving his people; it includes an assertion of his sole Sovereignty, proclaiming repeatedly: "I am the LORD, there is no other." He declares also that his regime of managing and maintaining his creations, especially his chosen ones, is just and upright. This loud declaration brought happiness as well as hurting to his chosen ones; it sounded good because at a time when they were being enslaved and tortured in their exile, it also signaled to the bizarre action of their Lord. They were bewildered and shocked by his prophecy that he would deliver them from exile and bring them to their own land not through any one of their clan who are supposed to be the only righteous under the sun, but by a pagan king Cyrus.

In addition to Cyrus, Prophet Ezekiel spells out the good deeds of two more pagan kings, Darius and Artaxerxes, who, joining together, brought liberation and restoration of the chosen ones under the anointing of the Creator (Ez. 6:7ff). They generously decreed that the Temple should be built and Jewish people should be permitted to worship their God as they wanted. Therefore the chosen ones were glad and esteemed the kings as good persons though they were pagan kings. Yet they never accepted that these kings would go to heaven!

Only God is to be the supreme master of all. He is the sole master whom humans should obey. He is the beginning and the end of our lives. All the persons, whether they are leaders or lovers, elders or friends, and any helpers that come in between God and us are only his candidates, his appointees, his choices, and his stewards. They can be anybody; they may appear like our enemies; they may be strangers, pagans, communists, Democrats, Republicans, environmentalists, racial supremacists, and fundamentalists. They are indeed chosen by the God of justice either for our blessing or for our punishment or chastisement.

By this unique action, God informs his people that no one may challenge his freedom and individuality, especially in his saving deeds of justice, mercy, and fidelity. He upholds his power to choose any person for his work: they can come from the east and west, north and south; they can be sinful adulterers, public sinners, criminals hanging on the cross. Even if the chosen ones keep silent, the stones will be stirred to cry out "Hosanna" to his beloved Son (Luke 19:40). God has his sole hands to pick out his representatives in his own wisdom and self-determination to accomplish either his just deeds of punishment and purification or his merciful works of salvation and restoration. Indeed, as he confirms, "there is no just and saving God but him" (Isa. 45:21).

Knowing fully well of this unfathomable nature of God, disciples like Paul (Rom. 9) preached relentlessly that no human, being a clay, is worth enough to talk back to God, who is the Potter, saying, why have you created me so? When the same God recreates the vessels of wrath into vessels of mercies, no one can dare enough to question his action. While our God was patiently enduring the humans' frivolous and perverted behavior for years, suddenly if he permits some evils to purify us and revive us, we don't have any say in it. The worst instance would be that when our God, whom we try to please by our external practices, chooses some alien, some person, like King Cyrus, who is not of our race, our color, our caste, our group, is brought by him to realize his just and merciful cause in our midst, we cannot question his whacky action.

This is our God brought to us by the Word incarnate. Amen, that is the only word we can say and salute our just, merciful, and faithful God.

God's Immeasurable Mercy Is Conditioned by His Justice

The unconditional mercy of God is eternally conditioned by his justice. Scriptures insist on this unthinkable fact existing in God. Holy men and women of the past and of the present never fail to recall every day of their lives that their God is both just and merciful. In Psalm 143, David sings to the Lord: "Do not enter into judgment with your servant; before you no one can be just . . . In the morning let me hear of your mercy." He repeatedly names this character of God as "righteousness" and "holiness."

Some years back, one of my friends, a cradle Catholic but who turned to be a strong atheist, wrote to me a poem in which he cried out the following:

> God, when my brothers were victims of Holocaust where were you?
> God, when my friends were crucified and burned by Inquisition where were you?
> God, when my colleagues were slaves, where were you?
> God, when my sisters were and still are being mistreated where are you?

The poem did not stop there. It had twenty more lines pointing out the historical "eternal silence" of God in calamities and atrocities faced by the humans. My friend thought he was beating my faith down by his cynical remarks about God. But I wrote him back that he was not saying anything new and I have been questioning God every morning in a similar tone when I wake up. The only difference is that unlike my friend, I add always a footnote to my questions: "Still, not my will but let yours be done."

All the questions of my friend and mine are not totally original. They are already found profusely in OT books, especially in those 150 psalms. These questions are perennial heartbeats of humans who are suffering from evil forces. Very astonishingly, the only standard answer we hear from the Lord to those questions and complaints throughout the centuries is the following: He loves us and therefore nothing will harm us. Everything that happens in the form of evil will still take us to his heavenly destiny.

God of love always tells us we are created in his likeness and image of love. That means we were made out of love, for love, and to love. Our origin is love and our destiny is love. When we pervert our intention, our dreams, our imagination, our ambition, our life from love to hatred, injustice, discrimination, and violence, we literally live in hell and try to include others to be burned too in that hell.

But the wise disciples of Jesus as we are will not allow those perpetrators of evil to prevail over us. To assist in our efforts, Jesus, presenting to us our God as the most compassionate Prodigal Father, insists, "Be compassionate as your heavenly Father is compassionate." The same Father inspired his Son to forgive his enemies and even made him pray for them. He revealed that those who suffer from evil forces are not alone. He is also suffering with them, weeps with them, encourages his other sons and daughters to join in hands to assist them. If need be, He joins with his people in waging wars against evil forces. He was always on their side to win those wars.

We must hear daily the following comforting words of our loving God, very specially during those days of inner and outer wars that we fight: "I am who am. I can only be what I am to be. I am the Father of a prodigal family. I am the Lord of Love and compassion. I am just love. That is my justice. My punishment for all those evil things my sons and daughters do is only my love. I am capable of killing those perpetrators of evil only through my love. Those who follow me in love will find my love as heaven. Surely those who don't acknowledge it will experience my love as their hell" (an unknown author's inspiration quoted in my book *Daily Dose Reflections* for September 10).

Our merciful and just God deals with all of his humans as a school principal does to her students. A boy was sent by his teacher to the principal's office for misbehaving in class. After hearing the facts, the principal took out a ledger and wrote the boy's name in it. As she did so, she said, "You have not been sent to me before and I don't know you very well. You may be a good student for all I know. At times, even good students make mistakes. Therefore, I'll make a note in pencil that you were sent here today and I'll also make note of the reason you were sent. But as you can see, I'm entering this note in pencil, and I'm not bearing down very hard. If you behave and are not sent to see me for the rest of the year, I will erase this from the ledger and no one will ever know anything about it." This was a lesson in mercy that the boy never forgot.

Our holy God behaves this way millions of times in humans' lives. Actually when we fall down to the pit of sinfulness, he offers us a long rope of waiting, tolerating, and patiently enduring hurts we usually inflict on his kindheartedness. He acts as a Prodigal Father toward his younger son or like the Gardener toward the barren tree. It is left to our proficiency to make the best or worst use of every time God bestows the chance of his bottomless mercy to climb up from our bottomless pit. Charles G. Coleman very aptly explains the human cooperation with the mercy of God in his book *That Voice Behind You*: "God's mercy is like the potential energy of water in a pipe, which can act only when a human hand turns the faucet."

It is wrong to speak of God's need of love from His creation, but remember how God himself expressed his longing for that love: like a father starved for some response, any response, from his rebellious children; like a jilted lover who, against all reason, gives his faithless beloved one more chance. These are the images God summoned up again and again throughout the time of the prophets. The deepest longings we feel on earth, as parents, as lovers, are mere flickers of the hungering desire God feels for us.

I have heard and read so many sermons and homilies about the "rare blend" secret of God's CHESED consisting of justice, mercy, and fidelity. I don't think nothing would compete the sermon I caught sight of in the book of Deuteronomy chapter 32. It is a sort of poetic sermon by Moses describing the Lord's marvelous deeds of CHESED. Comparing God as the Rock, Moses proclaims his mercy, justice, and fidelity:

> For I will proclaim the name of the LORD,
> praise the greatness of our God! The Rock—
> how faultless are his deeds, how right all his
> ways! A faithful God, without deceit, just and
> upright is he! (3-4)

The sermon reminds Israelites how the Creator dealt with them as a gracious Father, who brought them out of darkness and slavery, and how he supported them in everyday life. Remember the days of old; consider the years of generations past. Ask your father, he will inform you, your elders, they will tell you . . . But the LORD's portion was his people; his allotted share was Jacob. He found them in a wilderness, a wasteland of howling desert.

He shielded them, cared for them, guarded them as the apple of his eye. As an eagle incites its nestlings, hovering over its young, so he spread his wings, took them, bore them upon his pinions. The LORD alone guided them, no foreign god was with them. He had them mount the summits of the land, fed them the produce of its fields" (7–13).

Such a merciful and kind God, as Moses exposes, was to behave with those hardheaded people to correct their unjust and ungrateful attitude and behavior against him. Exalting the immense power of God's justice in his own human way, Moses shouted out that God's CHESED would avenge the blood of his servants and take vengeance on his foes.

> They forsook the God who made them and scorned the Rock of their salvation . . . They sacrificed to demons, to "no-gods" . . . The LORD saw and was filled with loathing, provoked by his sons and daughters. He said, I will hide my face from them, and see what becomes of them . . . For they are a fickle generation, children with no loyalty in them! (16–20)

The just God did as he revealed. He permitted the people, who were unfaithful to his CHESED, to undergo terrible sufferings and pains. God's HESED behaved in an unthinkable way as usual. Instead of directly punishing his people, he used another strange scheme: "I will incite them with a 'no-people'; with a foolish nation I will provoke them" (21b). However, CHESED never closed its chapter that grim way. Moses ends his sermon with a joyful note. He explains about another strange and unfathomable CHESED deed of God who demonstrated his eternal and enduring mercy by smiting those foreign invaders who had done harm to his people.

> See now that I, I alone, am he, and there is no god besides me. It is I who bring both death and life, I who inflict wounds and heal them . . . and my hand lays hold of judgment, With vengeance I will repay my foes and requite those who hate me. (39–41).

CHAPTER 7

The Enduring Fidelity of
the Merciful, Just God

Faithfulness is one of the three attributes of God that are embedded in his CHESED as well as that which deeply and personally affect humans. Holy Scriptures testify to its innate existence in God, never fading or broken eternally. I tried to count the references on this fact in the Bible. Getting help from various preachers and writers, so far I have discovered 270 verses. Certainly there may be more.

My point here is why to such trouble would God, as well as the sacred writers, take to repeatedly emphasize this attribute besides justice and mercy. It is simply because both parties were fully aware of the limitations of humans in responding to the CHESED covenant they made with their Master. Like David, sinful but always begging and finding mercy from his Creator, these sacred writers have encountered God's enduring faithfulness first in their personal lives and second as seen also among their people. Invariably, in most of his Psalms, David has included many references on such experiential truth:

> I will establish his dynasty forever, his throne
> as the days of the heavens. If his descendants
> forsake my teaching, do not follow my
> decrees, if they fail to observe my statutes, do
> not keep my commandments, I will punish
> their crime with a rod and their guilt with
> blows. But I will not take my mercy from him,
> nor will I betray my bond of faithfulness. I
> will not violate my covenant; the promise of
> my lips I will not alter. By my holiness I swore
> once for all. I will never be false to David.
> (Ps. 89)

David repeats untiringly his indomitable faith in God's faithfulness toward his covenantal relationship with humans. For example, in Psalm 100, a hymn inviting the people to enter the Temple courts with thank offerings for the God who created them, David sings, "Good indeed is the LORD, his mercy endures forever, and his faithfulness lasts through every generation" (100:5). In Psalm 57, while he highlights the greatness of God's fidelity, he also begs for the same from God, and in addition he asserts his will and wish of being steadfast:

> For your mercy towers to the heavens; your
> faithfulness reaches to the skies. (11)

> May God send fidelity and mercy! (4)

Besides, sacred authors have discovered a large chasm existing between God and his covenantal party, the humans, for instance, in the following texts:

> If we are unfaithful he remains faithful, for he cannot deny himself. (2 Tim. 2:13)

> God is not a human being who speaks falsely, nor a mortal, who feels regret. Is God one to speak and not act, to decree and not bring it to pass? (Num. 23:19)

> What if some were unfaithful? Will their infidelity nullify the fidelity of God? (Rom. 3:3)

Calling his people with love as sons and spelling out how they were utterly ignorant of him and his deeds, God heartbrokenly complains,

> Sons have I raised and reared, but they have rebelled against me! An ox knows its owner, and an ass, its master's manger; But Israel does not know, my people has not understood. Ah! Sinful nation, people laden with wickedness, evil offspring, corrupt children! They have forsaken the LORD, spurned the Holy One of Israel, apostatized . . . The whole head is sick, the whole heart faint. From the sole of the foot to the head there is no sound spot in it. (Isa. 1:1-31)

From all those biblical verses, we come to know what an immeasurable gap there is between the two parties of the CHESED covenant: While God is truthful, humans are liars; while God is honest, humans are deceitful;

while God is single-minded, humans are double-minded; while humans are wishy-washy, God is steadfast; and while God's faithfulness is enduring, the humans' is very fluctuating.

There is also another valid reason for the frequent citations in the Bible on the faithfulness of God. On the part of God, together with his justice, God is so bended "bottomlessly" in his mercy, and he longs for his other party to return back to him and reconcile with his covenant. On the other side is the perverted and lost, but then the converted humans yearn for God's forgiveness and his parental hug. Hence, God the faithful, just, and merciful has taken an unthinkable step of promising to send a Messiah to atone all of humans' sins and that which he fulfilled through his beloved Son Jesus. This has been the most life-changing faithful act of God by which the entire human race benefitted.

In writing about God's faithful deeds, the writer of the letter to the Hebrews (6:18) says that it is impossible for God to lie in two immutable things, namely, the promise and the oath he made to his people. Faithfulness in God is proven unconditional: No second party can influence his designs and deeds both positively and negatively; his CHESED-based covenant is the one and only element that programs all of his actions. If any human would freely and sincerely plan to please God, they must be faith-filled. That is what the sacred writer of the letter to the Hebrews writes (11:6). To expound the word *faith*, the writer uses one whole chapter in his letter (11), telling us that it means first to uphold an undoubted conviction and hope on the unseen things, mainly the existence of our invisible God and his abundant rewards waiting for those who seek him. Faith means trusting in the CHESED character of God before we see how He is going to work things out. He has given us His Word, and His promises still stand.

Secondly, faith also indicates an obstinate steadfastness in our earnest efforts to fulfill the covenantal promises we make to God. To augment the second dimension of our faith, the Letter lists out so many witnesses from the history who have become our role models in this matter. Thus, we find an intrinsic connection between faith and faithfulness, which can be also termed "faith-filled" life. And this is why we repeatedly sing our own experiential faith in God's fidelity God keeps his word from age to age, His word is with us to the end of days (ref. Stanbrook Abbey Hymnal).

The Faithful God's Eternal Longing

Many among us most of the time complain against God's staggering demands from us, especially sacred authors who underline about God's perennial call or his wakeup calls for humans' fidelity and that too as he is. "Be perfect as your heavenly Father is perfect." He too threatens us with agonizing punishment for our infidelity, saying, "This people's heart goes astray; they do not know my ways. Therefore I swore in my anger: They shall never enter my rest" (Ps. 95:10–11). And so we blame that he acts always bossy and never bother about our limitations.

This kind of thought is, though understandable, very absurd. It is understandable because we the humans, especially born and bred in this civilized age, are very much shaped and motivated by what modern philosophers call "the postmodern individuality." Being swayed by this sophisticated individualism, our hearts and minds cry out within us: "Do your own thing." "Make choices according to your thirst, baby." Such a wrongly formulated spirit is being venerated by us as modern civilized conscience, natural humanism, self-respect and pure liberty and freedom, and so on. This is why we hate laws and regulations; we are proud to disobey and violate them. Worse than the adults, young people are very hostile to laws and rules as they consider these laws "limiting their freedom." As the pope always decries, youngsters seek more low-cost happiness not only by ignoring and being careless but also by violating these laws. For them, the only thing that stands on the way to happiness is the lack of freedom; they feel that obedience to laws infringes their licentiousness; any law that curtails freedom is to be rejected. They think how much happier life would be without so many do's and don'ts!

However, the same modern brainwave is absurd if we reflect a little bit on the behavior and his deeds as handed down to us by Scriptures and tradition. As we discussed earlier in detail, God cannot go against his nature—a nature that is made of justice, mercy, and fidelity. Secondly, the factual truth of his demands will emerge from his manifesto on them. Generally, the Bible calls all God's demands to us as laws. I love to portray the laws of God by a popular term: They are optional instructional manuals for our successful and blessed life. It is God's eternal design for us that by walking continually in the way of his "instructions," we may never be deceived or misled.

From a book about the life of St. John Berchmans, I picked up one most important guideline mainly for life in my youth. It is an axiom he used to live by and also to share with all his friends: "Keep the rule and the rule will keep you." That has been ringing up to this day in my mind as a valuable guide.

That is how God clarified through Moses his reason for his law-binding demands.

> See, I have today set before you, life and good, death and evil. If you obey the commandments of the LORD, your God, which I am giving you today, loving the LORD, your God, and walking in his ways, and keeping his commandments, statutes and ordinances, you will live and grow numerous, and the LORD, your God, will bless you in the land you are entering to possess. If, however, your heart turns away and you do not obey, but are led astray and bow down to other gods and serve them, I tell you today that you will certainly perish; you will not have a long life on the land which you are crossing the Jordan to enter and possess. (Deut. 30:15–18)

Explaining a little more of what Moses wrote about God's manifesto, the Grand Teacher Sirach instructs us: "If you choose you can keep the commandments, they will save you; if you trust in God, you too shall live; he has set before you fire and water to whichever you choose, stretch forth your hand. Before man, are life and death, good and evil, whichever he chooses shall be given him!" (Sir. 15:15–17).

Historically, we know that so many humans who were sincere to strive for a joy-filled and peaceful life in this world have been fully aware of this option God has entrusted to them. They have strenuously tried to fulfill God's demands shown as his practical manual of instruction. Among those numerous witnesses, I can pick one who has been the archetypical person, King David. If we go through his poetic creations as Psalms, he is seen overwhelmed with the importance and necessity of the "demands of God," giving many names to them, such as *statute*, *commandment*, *precept*, *testimony*, *word*, *judgment*, *way*, and *promise*. This is specifically found in his Psalm 119, which is made of 176 verses filled with appreciations for God's laws as an instructional manual for human life. David also in his other hymns spells out his thirst for living a faithful life in front of God, but being aware of his weakness, he adds an ejaculatory prayer with similar verses as "My heart is steadfast, God, my heart is steadfast" (Ps. 57:8).

Jesus, being David's Son, expressed in his life such enthusiasm for faithfully living up to God's demands. He named them as "God's will." In talking about faith, he never missed to include the adjective *enduring*, *steadfast*, and *audacious* to emphasize his disciples to be "faithful" as their heavenly Father is "faithful." Discussing about the end of humanity, he declared, "Whoever endures to the end will be saved" (Matt. 10:22). Foreseeing the humans' treacherous infidelity, he too sounded frustrated and sad, saying, "When the Son of Man comes, will he find faith on earth?" (Luke 18:8).

CHAPTER 8

CHESED of God Related to His Holiness

In the previous chapter, we described that the attribute of justice is the core in God's CHESED dealings. Most people consider his justice to take its full form from his mighty kingship as judge, rewarder, and punisher. But above all, Scriptures underline that God's justice originates out of his nature of holiness and truthfulness.

God is the Holy One; he cannot go against his own nature of truth, justice, mercy, and fidelity. Therefore in his covenantal deals with humans, he is to be wholesome, and consequently, humans must be blessed and obliged by God's utter holiness. In this covenantal relationship, many of God's messengers and chosen ones have been inspired by the Lord how he is immensely holy. He deliberately demonstrated his holiness not only by his words and also by deeds. When he appeared to Moses in the burning bush, he stopped Moses from coming near him with his dirty sandals, warning him,

> Do not come near! Remove your sandals from
> your feet, for the place where you stand is holy
> ground. (Exod. 3:5)

> When the tabernacle is to move on, the Levites shall take it down; when the tabernacle is to be pitched, it is the Levites who shall set it up. Any unauthorized person who comes near it shall be put to death. (Num. 1:51)

As translators note, wherever the Hebrew word translated "comes near" in this context, it points out to someone unauthorized who intrudes upon the space set apart as holy. The Prophet Isaiah was bestowed a heavenly vision where he saw and encountered the host of angels ceaselessly singing loudly: "Holy, holy, holy is the LORD of hosts! All the earth is filled with his glory!" (Isa. 6:1-4). They were inspired by the Creator to proclaim to his people his unquenchable ambition that his name should be called holy and asked his messengers to command his people to be as holy as he is (Lev. 19:2). They never cease to sing with David the awesome name of God as "Holy is he!" (Ps. 99).

Among all the attributes or characteristics of God, the Bible exposes to us the most significant one that identifies him very accurately, which is his holiness. It is the character that sets him apart from all created beings. It is not only the core of all his attributes but also it incorporates them within it. We also can say it is the root of all his other virtues or qualities such as his justice, his mercy, his faithfulness, and so on.

In order to explain God's holiness fully when the sacred authors write about it, they also add to it his other attributes as much as they can. When the Psalmist, for instance, as we mentioned earlier, sings recurrently about

God's holiness in his Psalm 99, in tandem he attests about his justice:

> O mighty king, lover of justice, you have established fairness; you have created just rule in Jacob; (4) also he states with unction: O LORD, our God, you answered them (Israelites); you were a forgiving God to them. (8)

Holiness in biblical language means "wholeness." To be holy as our God is holy, we need to be wholeheartedly be of God. The first and the greatest of all his commandments to us, as Jesus confirmed, is the following: "You shall love the LORD, your God, with your whole heart, and with your whole being, and with your whole strength" (Deut. 6:5; Matt. 22:37).

The call of God in Jesus to holiness is very radical, demanding from us a total and holistic surrender of everything we are, our loves, our identities, and our very self. This is what Jesus intended to call us for his discipleship. "Whoever wishes to come after me must deny himself, take up his cross, and follow me. For whoever wishes to save his life will lose it, but whoever loses his life for my sake and that of the gospel will save it" (Mark 8:34–35).

Many of us wrongly perceive that to be holy means to be morally pure. And therefore they look through and explain God's holiness as his moral purity. Yes, good morality is included into the holiness, but only secondarily. God certainly is all-good and all-pure. There is no guile in him as some religions have concocted stories about him; though the sacred writers had used those terms, parables, and events as found in religious traditions at their times in describing to us about our God, for instance, "he was angry," "he cursed," "he cruelly punished," and so on, they never alluded his deeds of justice toward angels or humans to the products of his dark side. It was the authors' intention of portraying God's justice-filled acts when his holiness and truth are maligned and denigrated by his creatures. It is his nature to desist such blasphemous acts found among his chosen ones. Moral goodness is intrinsically embedded in his nature as goodness and truth.

God's Justice Originated from His Holiness and Truth

In the previous chapter, we described the attribute of justice as the core in his CHESED dealings. Most people consider his justice to take its full form from his mighty Kingship as judge, rewarder, and punisher. But above all, Scriptures underline God's justice as originating out of his nature of holiness and truthfulness. Richard L. Strauss wrote,

> *God's righteousness (or justice) is the natural expression of His holiness. If He is infinitely pure, then He must be opposed to all sin, and that opposition to sin must be demonstrated in His treatment of His creatures. When we read that God is righteous or just, we are being assured that His actions toward us are in perfect agreement with His holy nature. (The Joy of Knowing God [Neptune, New Jersey: Loizeaux Brothers, 1984], p. 140)*

Those words of Richard Strauss bring us very close to a concise definition of righteousness. Righteousness, in relation to men, is the conformity to a standard. Unlike men, God is not subject to anything outside of Himself. All religious Scriptures in the world proclaim in unison that God the Supreme Spiritual Being is holy and so in the Bible all sacred authors join with Prophet Isaiah in audibly but spiritually hearing in their inner sanctuaries the chorus of angels singing to God, "Holy, Holy, Holy is the Lord of hosts!" (Isa. 6:3). They were inspired by the Creator to proclaim to his people his unquenchable ambition that his name should be called holy and asked his messengers to command his people to be as holy as he is (Lev. 19:2). They never cease to sing with David the awesome name of God as "Holy is he!" (Ps. 99).

Among all the attributes or characteristics of God, the Bible exposes to us the most significant one that identifies him very accurately, which is his holiness. It is the character that sets him apart from all created beings. It is not only the core of all his attributes but also it incorporates them within it. We also can say it is the root of all his other virtues or qualities, such as his justice, his mercy, his faithfulness, and so on. In order to explain God's holiness fully when the sacred authors write about it, they also add to it his other attributes as much as they can. When the Psalmist, for instance, as we mentioned earlier, sings recurrently about God's holiness in his Psalm 99, in tandem he attests about his justice:

> O mighty king, lover of justice, you have established fairness; you have created just rule in Jacob; (4) also he states with unction: O LORD, our God, you answered them

(Israelites); you were a forgiving God to
them. (8)

Holiness in biblical language means "wholeness." To be
holy as our God is holy, we need to wholeheartedly be of
God. The first and the greatest of all his commandments
to us, as Jesus confirmed, is as follows: "You shall love the
LORD, your God, with your whole heart, and with your
whole being, and with your whole strength" (Deut. 6:5;
Matt. 22:37). The call of God in Jesus to holiness is very
radical, demanding from us a total and holistic surrender
of everything we are, our loves, our identities, and our
very self. This is what Jesus intended to call us for his
discipleship. "Whoever wishes to come after me must deny
himself, take up his cross, and follow me. For whoever
wishes to save his life will lose it, but whoever loses his
life for my sake and that of the gospel will save it" (Mark
8:34–35).

Many of us wrongly perceive that to be holy means
to be morally pure. And therefore they look through
and explain God's holiness as his moral purity. Yes,
good morality is included into the holiness, but only
secondarily. God certainly is all-good and all-pure. There
is no guile in him as some religions have concocted
stories about him; though the sacred writers had used
those terms, parables, and events as found in religious
traditions at their times in describing to us about our
God, for instance, "he was angry," "he cursed," "he cruelly
punished," and so on, they never alluded his deeds of
justice toward angels or humans to the products of his
dark side. It was the authors' intention of portraying God's
justice-filled acts when his holiness and truth are maligned

and denigrated by his creatures. It is his nature to desist such blasphemous acts found among his chosen ones.

Moral goodness is intrinsically embedded in his nature as goodness and truth. Primarily, it is about our intrinsic and conscious union with God in Jesus. Pure life and moral behavior are only its outward expressions by our humble and grateful services. As Joel Scandrett, an Anglican priest and adjunct instructor of theology at Wheaton College, wrote in one of his articles "Holy to the Core" in *Christianity Today*, "basically, our holiness of attitude and behavior is nothing but our fidelity as that of God's Faithfulness, our merciful and just thoughts, words and actions which God expects from us in keeping with his ideal justice and mercy."

Such a discussion on the holiness of God contributes lavishly to our understanding of scriptural use of CHESED. The most fundamental connotation of scriptural verses like "Be holy because God is holy" and "Be merciful as your heavenly Father is merciful" are not merely a code of good and pure conduct in human life and, consequently, humans live and move peacefully and securely in social life; but much more it, those words declare a breathtaking policy we have to take in our relationship with the Almighty. The main assertion of God is as follows: "You, humans, are my creations; I have chosen you out of nothing to be exclusively set apart only for me; you should dedicate yourself therefore to me as my personal property or heritage. I will be your God and you will be my people" (ref. Lev. 26:12; Heb. 8:10; 1 Pet. 1:16). God is the Holy One and the Creator of human life, and the human being is blessed and obliged by God's utter holiness.

Therefore, every human life is holy, sacrosanct, and inviolable. Holiness is a truth that pervades the whole of the Old Covenant. In this covenantal relationship, many of God's messengers and chosen ones have been inspired by the Lord's being immensely holy. He deliberately demonstrated his holiness not only by his words but also by deeds. When he appeared to Moses in the burning bush, he stopped Moses from coming near him with his dirty sandals, warning him,

> Do not come near! Remove your sandals from your feet, for the place where you stand is holy ground. (Exod. 3:5)

> When the tabernacle is to move on, the Levites shall take it down; when the tabernacle is to be pitched, it is the Levites who shall set it up. Any unauthorized person who comes near it shall be put to death. (Num. 1:51)

As translators note, wherever the Hebrew word translated "comes near" in this context, it points out to someone unauthorized who intrudes upon the space set apart as holy. Prophet Isaiah was bestowed a heavenly vision where he saw and encountered the host of angels ceaselessly singing loudly: "Holy, holy, holy is the LORD of hosts! All the earth is filled with his glory!" (Isa. 6:1–4).

Holiness is in God, and only from God can it pass to the crown of God's creation: human beings. We are made in the image and likeness of God, and God's holiness, his "total otherness" is imprinted on each one of us. Human beings become vehicles and instruments of God's holiness for the world. God is holy and calls all to holiness. The Mosaic Law exhorted, "You shall be holy; for I the Lord your God am holy" (Lev. 19:2). This holiness is the fire of God's Word that must be alive and burning within our hearts. It is this fire, this dynamism that will burn away the evil within us and around us and cause holiness to burst forth, healing and transforming the society and culture surrounding us. Evil is only eradicated by holiness, not by harshness.

Holiness introduces into society a seed that heals and transforms. This loaded statement describes best the vocation of every man and woman and the entire mission of the church throughout history: a call to holiness.

Holiness is a way of life that involves commitment and activity. It is not a passive endeavor, but rather a continuous choice to deepen one's relationship with God and to then allow this relationship to guide all of one's actions in the world. Holiness requires a radical change in mind-set and attitude. The acceptance of the call to holiness places God as our final goal in every aspect of our lives. This fundamental orientation toward God even envelops and sustains our relationship with other human beings. Sustained by a life of virtue and fortified by the gifts of the Holy Spirit, God draws us ever closer to himself and to that day when we shall see Him face-to-face in heaven and achieve full union with him. Here and now, we can find holiness in our personal experience of putting forth our best efforts in the workplace, patiently raising our children, and building good relationships at home, at school, and at work. If we make all of these things a part of our loving response to God, we are on the path to holiness. God's holiness constitutes an essential imperative for the moral behavior. In this sense, there have been countless men and women throughout our Christian tradition who can be named the true "revolutionaries of holiness," as Pope Benedict XVI said so beautifully during the 2005 World Youth Day in Cologne, Germany.

CHAPTER 9

Eternal Celebration of CHESED

Whenever I am impelled by my Christian spirit to approach God for forgiveness by humble confession of my sins, I join the club of postmodern rationalists to question myself, why should I do? As a second thought, I feel that in human life, victory does not always come at the first step. World history testifies to it. Numerous political, religious, social leaders as well as world celebrities achieved their successes in each one's field of dreams ever at their first action. And God in Scriptures ever contend that he grants our request or approves our plan of action at our first "knocking his door."

The same is true with our failings to respond to God's mercy in our discipleship. A spiritual author, Charles G. Coleman, writes about it very succinctly:

> There is little evidence in scripture to suggest that God's plan for the Christian life is a single unchangeable blueprint, or that failure dooms one to a second-best life. On the contrary, the concern of Bible writers seems to be that we should confess our mistakes to

God, and learn from them, so we can serve
Him more wisely.

Hence, we can boldly declare that the Bible we handle
is a "Good Book of Mercy," in the sense that it is the
"First Book of our Second Chance." Humans' final resort
is God's just mercy. Dr. William Carey was a British
missionary, a Particular Baptist minister, a translator, and
an activist. He also opened the first university in India
offering degrees. He is known as the "father of modern
missions." Becoming an expert in Indian languages,
such as Sanskrit, Hindi, etc., he translated the Bible into
those languages. He lived for forty-three years with people
ravaged by extreme poverty and diseases. He has been
esteemed as a social reformer and an illustrious Christian
missionary by biographers; he was also criticized for
being a "colonial ideologue with prejudice, hyperbole and
concealed racism."

As any human, he had his ups and downs in his
personal and family life. When he was suffering from a
dangerous illness, the inquiry was made: "If this sickness
should prove fatal, what passage would you select as the
text for your funeral sermon?" He replied, "Oh, I feel
that such a poor sinful creature is unworthy to have
anything said about him; but if a funeral sermon must
be preached, let it be from the words, 'Have mercy upon
me, O God, according to Thy loving kindness; according
unto the multitude of Thy tender mercies blot out my
transgressions." In the same spirit of humility, he directed
in his will that the following inscription and nothing
more should be cut on his gravestone:

WILLIAM CAREY
BORN AUGUST 17th, 1761
DIED ——

A wretched, poor, and helpless worm
On Thy kind arms I fall.

Only true children of God cry for mercy upon their unprofitableness. If we need God's mercy from the Lord for our good works, our prayers, our preaching, our almsgivings, and our holiest things, let us imagine how much more we require it when we are conscious of our sinfulness!

The Bible portrays our eternal destiny as an unending sumptuous banquet that is altogether different from what we enjoy in our parties. God hosts in his kingdom the banquet of his mercy, love, compassion, and forgiveness and joy. It is amazing to read in the Bible how God spends not only his timeless time in his heavenly abode but also his "Emmauelic" time among humans. Jesus indicates (Luke 15:1-32) that God's one and only preoccupation is celebrating joyfully, preparing sumptuous meals of joy, peace, forgiveness, and inviting and waiting for and waiting on as well on all of his human creatures at his table. The occasion of greatest enjoyment in God's heavenly celebration is when his enduring mercy bestows forgiveness to sinners.

Joy breeds joy. When we believe that God has forgiven and accepted us into his banquet chamber, this conviction makes us rejoice and celebrate our every minute joyfully as the younger prodigal son did. Unfortunately, there are too many among us who lose, like the elder son, such noble moments; they have forgotten or ignored the genuine source of joy, namely, God's mercy. There are too many among us who feel like the elder son who are complacent in what we hold in life today. We are content with what we perform as religious observances, but we never have time to look into how with our relationship with our God. We may apparently stay inside the house of the Father but very sadly like the elder son would be far distant from the heart of the Father. Our real rest and joy is to be very closely connected to how we relate to God's bountiful mercy. "The grace of our Lord has been abundant, along with the faith and love that are in Christ Jesus. Christ Jesus came into the world to save sinners" (1 Tim. 7:12–17).

Recently, I came across a saying posted online in a blog: "Only God is in the position to look down on anyone." Some readers appreciated it, telling it was a meaningful, striking, and highlighting verse about the superiority of God. I thought they missed the real background of the verb "look down." Looking down may mean two different attitudes of the doer: When people look down on somebody, it denotes their superiority complex, arrogance, hatred, or aversion. If God looks down on humans, it indicates that out of mercy he stoops down to them—condescending, deigning, patronizing, bending down, leaning on the needy who call upon him. Our God is always a merciful Supreme. Even though God may hold such immense power and position, he stoops down on us not on the basis of some age-old profile system but purely out of his bountiful mercy.

Our Merciful God first and last sees our intent, not as we judge others but only by deeds. As angels sang at the birth of Jesus, "peace to people of good will," God's mercy is exclusively for those who want to do good, yet fall into the temptations of sin. In a homily, Pope Francis is quoted as saying, "We do the work of God on earth; because He does His work through us." He echoed Saint Augustine who wrote, 'Without God, we cannot. Without us, God will not."

I once read in an online blog: "God's telephone number is Jeremiah 33:3—Call on me, and I will answer you, and show you great and mighty things, which you do not know." This is why so many of my mentors advised me on repeating the words of Dr. William Carey: "Expect great things from God; attempt great things for God."

SECTION III

Jesus, the Embodiment of God's CHESED

Elohim shall send forth His **chesed** *and His emes.*
—Psalm 57:(3)4, OJB

God will send his gracious love and truth.
—Psalm 57:(3)4, International Standard Version

Jesus claimed that he is the "Christ Messiah," he was "sent by God," his authority is "greater than that of Moses," he is the "Only Begotten Son of God," he is the "Light of the World," he is "the Way, the Truth, and the Life," and he is "the Gate" to enter into Eternal Kingdom, and so on. With all those claims, he included that he is the true image of the most amazing characteristic of God, namely, "merciful."

CHAPTER 10

Jesus, the Final Manifestation of God's CHESED

In his canticle, the high priest Zachariah, father of John the Baptizer, portrays the identity and mission of Jesus of Nazareth (Luke 1:69-75). Calling him "a horn of our salvation," he sings that Jesus was the fulfillment of God's promise of salvation to us from all our enemies, of showing mercy to our forebears, of being faithful to God's covenant. Jesus would grant us a fear-free situation in which we would worship God in holiness and righteousness all our days.

Very surprisingly in addition to the prophetic declaration of Zachariah about Jesus as Messiah of mercy and fidelity, his beloved son John the Baptizer surprisingly introduced Jesus at his arrival in public as a Doer of justice:

> I am baptizing you with water, but one mightier than I is coming. I am not worthy to loosen the thongs of his sandals. He will baptize you with the Holy Spirit and fire.

> His winnowing fan is in his hand to clear
> his threshing floor and to gather the wheat
> into his barn, but the chaff he will burn with
> unquenchable fire. (Luke 3:16–17)

The main reason for such statement about Jesus is John's careful reading of the OT Messianic prophecies with God's Spirit. Prophet Jeremiah wrote in his book an oracle of the Lord on the fulfillment of his promise to the Israel:

> In those days, at that time, I will make a just
> shoot spring up for David; he shall do what is
> right and just in the land. In those days Judah
> shall be saved and Jerusalem shall dwell safely;
> this is the name they shall call her: "The
> LORD our justice." (33:15–16)

Prophet Isaiah, on his part, detailed this oracle of God, which we will focus more in this book. Prophesying Jesus's coming to the world and calling him as the shoot sprouting from the stump of Jesse, he proclaimed Jesus's justice as derived from his Father:

> He shall judge the poor with justice and
> decide fairly for the land's afflicted. He shall
> strike the ruthless with the rod of his mouth,
> and with the breath of his lips he shall slay
> the wicked. Justice shall be the band around
> his waist, and faithfulness a belt upon his
> hips. (Isa. 11:1–5)

Jesus was the enfleshed CHESED of God, sent by God to judge the world justly and lead his followers toward the truth and righteousness. Scriptural passages never lose sight of the rare blending of mercy and justice uncompromisingly present both in God the Father and God the Son. In this prophecy, we can clearly notice Isaiah pointing out how the Messiah would perform his just deeds both among the poor as well as the wicked: "The poor will be judged fairly while the wicked would be slain by the breath of his mouth." In many OT books, we find the same approach to God's justice with mercy or his mercy with justice.

Almost all the biblical references on the divine justice, both in OT and NT, never miss to include that justice comes out of God's mercy. A suitable example in this regard is found in the book of Malachi and the Gospel of Luke. The oracle of Malachi talks about the arising of the "Sun of Justice" but with healing wings: "But for you who fear my name, the sun of justice will arise with healing in its wings" (Mal. 3:20).

Concurrently, this OT view of the coexistence of justice and mercy in God is also followed by NT authors who esteem Jesus, the enfleshed CHESED, as the replica of God's justice and mercy as well. For example, the Malachian oracle about the coming of the "Sun of Justice" has been interpreted in NT as a prophetic reference to Jesus's coming. While Luke construes the "Sun of Justice" as "the daybreak from on high," he too closely follows the biblical spirit, adding mercy to the shining daybreak of justice: "Because of the tender mercy of our God by which the daybreak from on high will visit us to shine on those who sit in darkness and death's shadow, to guide our feet into the path of peace" (Luke 1:78–79).

Undoubtedly, all NT authors uphold that the Lord Jesus was righteous (just). All their affirmations had been originated from the OT prophecies about the Messiah. Matthew writes in his narration of Jesus's baptism that he was fulfilling all righteousness (justice) (3:15); again he confirms his assertion through the dream of Pilate's wife (27:19), and Luke concedes Jesus's righteousness (justice) through the declaration of a centurion (23:47). Besides, all the letters of the Apostles testify to the truth that Jesus is a merciful Savior with justice, full of righteousness.

The truth of incarnation we uphold about our Leader Jesus points out the historical fact that God, not closing in on himself, opens himself for open dialogue with humanity and in their own terms, needs, and cultures. Thus, with all other attributes of his Father, Jesus becomes an embodiment of God's immense mercy that had obliterated the abyss of the infinite difference existing between the divine and humans; Jesus, the Mercy incarnated, is therefore a bridge between us and God and "bridge builder" between one another.

Jesus never compromised in his proclamation of his merciful self. He even identified himself as he and his Father as one in mercy. This he confirmed at the beginning of his public life in one of his maiden preachings at a synagogue (Luke 4:16–21). Reading from Prophet Isaiah a passage that enlisted the roles of God-sent messenger, he finally accentuated that "today this scripture passage is fulfilled in your hearing." People who were there as well as the entire humanity understood well that Jesus was referring to his own identity of mercy. He loudly proclaimed that he was the one whom God anointed to bring glad tidings to the poor, he was the one whom God sent to proclaim liberty to captives and recovery of sight to the blind, to let the oppressed go free, and to proclaim a year acceptable to the Lord."

In obeying his Father's will, Jesus lived through at every step of his life God's CHESED. For that, he paid a terrible and unfathomable price of humiliation, rejection, and self-immolation. Paul portrays this CHESED experience of Jesus:

> Jesus, though he was in the form of God, did not regard equality with God something to be grasped. Rather, he emptied himself, taking the form of a slave, coming in human likeness; and found human in appearance, he humbled himself, becoming obedient to death, even death on a cross. (Phil. 2:6–8)

From the Gospels, we are aware of how treacherous his earthly life was, full of humiliations that hurt him one by one. Like his Father, out of his CHESED to liberate his fellowmen as Paul indicates, first he was humiliated at his incarnation, owning a body that is fragile and vulnerable; second, at his deathbed, the Cross where his bruised and pierced body was nailed to despair, thirst, loneliness, betrayal, abandonment, calumny, and mockery; third, at the transference of his glory, reputation, and power to the sinful hands of his fellowmen as church. Such was the abnormality we find in Jesus's mercy. Thus the saying "as the Father, so the Son" was fully realized in Jesus's CHESED' undertakings.

If we analyze all the events in Jesus's life and his sayings, we will discover that the only Gospel he preached was that of CHESED. He never exhausted in emphasizing the compassionate dimension of God's character. There are so many events and sayings collected by the evangelists that portray this truth.

Let us take Luke 7:36–50. In this Gospel event, Luke points out how Jesus, out of his CHESED, became "the friend of sinners." The merciful love of Jesus for the sinful woman pushes her to approach. All that the sinner did in front of him was to demonstrate her contrition, her resoluteness to come out of the sinful situation. Jesus called it her faith. Plus, he did two important acts of CHESED: His right and uncompromised judgment and his immense mercy toward the shivering and shame-filled woman. When a human person judged wrongly against the lowly woman, he corrected him then and there in support of the contrite and humble person. At the same time, he, with all the power delegated to him by his Father, forgave her, meaning he freed her from the clutches of evils like sinfulness and public malice toward her human life.

As a result of her encounter with Jesus, the sinful woman began to live a new and better life. And she would travel farther down the road than any of those who were now judging her. By welcoming her as Jesus did and graciously accepting her, Jesus put wind in her sails. The woman had never experienced anything like this before. Jesus was the best person she had ever met. She was not only forgiven, but she was also loved by Jesus. By treating her with kindness, Jesus helped her to believe in her own goodness.

Jesus of Nazareth indicated himself as the fulfillment of the biblical CHESED "Do not think that I have come to abolish the law or the prophets. I have come not to abolish but to fulfill" (Matt. 5:17). While all the translations include the verb "to fulfill," Weymouth reads, "to give them their completion" and in God's Word, "to make them come true." Jesus never intended to deviate his way or his followers' life from observing the Creator's commands and advices; rather he first fulfilled every bit of it in his life and exhorted his followers to do the same. He revered them, loved them, obeyed them, and brought them to fruition.

In that process of revisiting and renovating the law's understanding and observing, Jesus liberated the eternal validity of God's law from the humans' twisted and sometimes perverted interpretations and observances of it. For instance, he has unfolded its spiritual essence, its inward perfection. Not even a tad bit of the ceremonial law has passed away, if we regard the Mosaic Law as a whole. He didn't come to overthrow the law and the prophets or render them vain, but he came to unfold them, to personify them in living form, and to cherish them in the reverence, affection, and character of humans. He proposed to his Disciples only one purpose for observing the Law: that they should become perfect just as the Heavenly Father was (Matt. 5:48). In addition, he specified what God's perfection when he suggested to them to be merciful, just as the Heavenly Father is merciful (Luke 6:36). His only preoccupation in life was to educate his followers in this kind of approach toward interpreting and fulfilling the law and the prophets.

This mind-setup of Jesus became vivid when he was talking about all the rituals and rubrics being done in private and public forum. When he spoke of the law and the prophets, he referred to not just the Ten Commandments but also the entire spectrum of the Creator's directions and regulations as explicated in mainly the first five books of the Bible and all that the

OT prophets had written and lived with. In summary, we can list out the content of all those books that include the rule of action, which is generally designated by the term *conscience* or the capacity of being influenced by the moral relations of things; the long list of religious rites and ceremonies; the judicial laws, which directed the civil policy of the Hebrew nation; and the moral laws. These are summarized and named as the Ten Commandments, which are believed as the revealed will of God as to human conduct, binding on all men to the end of time. Jesus was convinced that his Father's only concern is how his human children are reciprocating his CHESED'. Therefore, when he was asked what was the greatest commandment given by God, he simply pointed out the CHESED (mercy, justice, and fidelity), which must be shown to God and the neighbors. "The whole Law and the prophets," he said, "depend on (hang on) these two commandments" (Matt. 22:36–40).

Matthew was one of those "public sinners" who then became the great Apostle of Jesus. He deliberately included in his Gospel (9:9–13) his story of forgiveness and election into Jesus's team that happened because of the mercy of Jesus. When he was called by Jesus and asked by the Master to host a party for him, the public was very much scandalized. Quoting from Hosea, the response of Jesus was a categorical manifesto about the core of his view about life, religion, and the law, namely, they are all the "mercy field" of the Creator: "Those who are well do not need a physician, but the sick do. Go and learn the meaning of the words, 'I desire mercy, not sacrifice. I did not come to call the righteous but sinners."

CHAPTER 11

———————

Jesus, the Refreshed CHESED of Man

CHESED of God, which is a rare blend of divine mercy, justice, and fidelity, has been the source and strength and ultimate aim of the old Israelites. Their leaders and prophets did their best to maintain it and stabilize it in the hearts of the people. At the arrival of Jesus, the God-sent Messiah, as we mentioned earlier, God's CHESED was seen walking in the midst of people in a very tangible and vivid form. All his actions and words were filled with CHESED in its paramount quality. He firmly believed that was his Father's will to send him to the world.

We too can ascertain that Jesus replenished and renewed the understanding and observing of the CHESED in the lives of his Disciples who have been dreaming to encounter "new heaven and new earth." He accomplished this venture first by his life, his death, and resurrection as well. The Gospels and the other NT writings are overflowing with testimonies and facts about how he fulfilled this mission. He was never tired of describing, expounding, and consequently instilling into the human hearts the amazing CHESED of his Father.

Being merciful to others is the only way, he underlined, to attain mercy from God; if we don't forgive others, he also insisted, the Father also will not forgive us. He also preached about how to maintain CHESED in our lives. While he underscored the importance of justice, he advised that first, to be just before God in fidelity, "repay to Caesar what belongs to Caesar and to God what belongs to God" (Luke 20:25). Also he reiterated the same, quoting Deuteronomy 6:4-5, that humans must wholeheartedly and totally love God (Mark 12:29-30). Simultaneously, he also pointed out the importance of showing justice to our fellowmen in fidelity, telling that we should love our neighbors as we love ourselves (Mark 12:31). He explained it a little more when he said, "Do to others whatever you would have them do to you (Matt. 7:12).

As much as he accentuated "showing justice toward God and neighbor," he heightened also the significance of mercy in fidelity. In comparing with the religious observances, he preferred "merciful acts." He developed this in two of his parables. One in the parable of the Pharisee and the tax collector (Luke 18:9-14), he depicted the prayer of mercy. "O God, be merciful to me" takes precedence to any sort of prayers in front of God. In the parable of the Good Samaritan (Luke 10:29-37), he portrayed that the Samaritan who performed merciful acts did a more excellent thing than those of the priest and of the Levite.

Besides his words, Jesus demonstrated his CHESED in active life, as Peter spoke (Acts 10:38), as he went about doing good. And Matthew details what good Jesus was performing (Matt. 9:35-36), writing, "Jesus went around to all the towns and villages, teaching in their synagogues, proclaiming the gospel of the kingdom, and curing every disease and illness. At the sight of the crowds, his heart was moved with pity for them because they were troubled and abandoned, like sheep without a shepherd."

Jesus's dream of living up to God's CHESED led him to the extent of facing ignominious death, death on the cross. He was conscious of the incredible resourcefulness of his death, which would become the first and the last and the best of all the sin offerings humans have been making to the God whom they fail by their infidelity.

This is what all Jesus's apostles and his prime disciples like Paul preached day in and day out. In the Letter to the Hebrews, we find the summary of their preaching (Heb. 2:14–18). The first effect from Jesus's death was that he might destroy the one who has the power of death, that is, the devil; second, that he might free those who through fear of death had been subject to slavery all their life; third, that he might be a merciful and faithful high priest before God to expiate the sins of the people; and fourthly, through what he suffered, he is able to help those who are being tested. The two-millennia church tradition continues to sing to the crucified Jesus on Good Friday with whole heart and mind and soul that "Lord, by your cross you saved the world."

CHAPTER 12

‑‑◈◉▶━━━━━━━━◈━━━━━━━━◀◉◈‑‑

Jesus's Gospel of the Resurrected CHESED

In the light of the Scriptures and the church teachings, we discover that Jesus, through his resurrection, fulfilled his CHESED, being faithful to his promise to his Father. Preaching about the inconceivable outcomes of resurrection of Jesus during Easter Mass of 2013, Pope Francis proclaimed, "Love has triumphed! Mercy has been victorious! God's mercy always triumphs!" He too added and affirmed that "the same merciful love, out of which the Son of God became man and led a life of humility and self-giving, has flooded Jesus's dead body with light and transfigured it, has made it pass into eternal life."

As for the aftermath results of resurrection, we witness not only in the time of Apostles but also in the church till this day that whoever visited or reflected over the empty tomb where Jesus had been buried and believed that his resurrection was a true but heavenly event in human history, they were historically empowered, renewed, rejuvenated, and began like freaks witnessing to the "resurrected mercy" of God in their daily lives.

Fulfilling his promise "I am with you always, until the end of the age" over the centuries, the risen Christ has been offering his followers how to conquer the evils of Satan who is always trying to distract humans from being faithful to God's mercy and justice. He continues to urge them to go beyond their self-centeredness, beyond their pride and hardheartedness, but to reach out to others living far and wide who are in need of spiritual, material, and social support.

The only testimony his followers have been transmitting was "we have encountered the resurrected Lord; he urged us to live and preach his Gospel of Mercy and Joy." Paul, one among those "freaks" of Jesus, reiterates in all his letters the real effects of Jesus's resurrection (Col. 3:1-4). Paul's claim is that through baptism, all followers of Christ are dead with him to unfaithful compromises of CHESED; instead, thanks to the resurrected Lord, they are raised with him to seek what is above and to persevere in the kind of "resurrected CHESED in their life, which is hidden with Christ. This means that all the merciful and just acts the followers of Jesus have accomplished in this world are spiritually sprouted out of the resurrected Lord who is spiritually present within them.

Through the Spirit of the resurrected Lord, his Disciples well understood the reality of Jesus's innovative love command. Ensuring to them "the old order has passed away. Behold, I make all things new" (Rev. 21:1-5), he presented God's CHESED in a very innovative way. He named God as Love, and if we have a bit of that love, we can make ourselves and our world all new. The "Love" he mentioned was a catchy and easily understandable term to humans. Thus, he changed the entire humans' love- approach topsy-turvy. He brought human love-based acts into the sanctuary of CHESED and consecrated them. Everything humans speak and act out of love can fully be turned out as a holy performance in AGAPE or CHESED-style.

While all that they perform as rituals, devotions, and prayers are focused on growing in esoteric spiritual love intimacy with God, they see to it that this interior love growth for God is magnified, witnessed, applied in earthly based love affairs in the midst of humans. Every love that comes from the hearts of these men and women as fathers, mothers, friends, sons, daughters, brothers, and sisters or as public servants takes a different form in Jesus. It's only through such of kind of lovers that the "new order" is managed and maintained in the world as Jesus longs for. That is nothing but his resurrection effect.

SECTION IV

Church Is Primarily a "Mercy" Home

Elohim shall send forth His **chesed** *and His emes.*
—Orthodox Jewish Bible

May God send fidelity and mercy!
—Psalm 57:4(3), NABRE

On the feast day of the bishop Saint Charles Borromeo, the church prays in the morning that the Lord would shape and renew her until she bears the image of Christ and shows his true likeness to the world. What is the true image and likeness of Christ that the church should bear? That is what we would be discussing in this section.

CHAPTER 13

Church Is a CHESED Dwelling on Earth

After stressing that our church identity and her origin come from the mercy, love, and grace of God (CHESED), Paul brings home to us that all those who are gathered and forming the church with no discrimination are one built together as God's dwelling. He writes to the Ephesians:

> So then you are no longer strangers and sojourners, but you are fellow citizens with the holy ones and members of the household of God, built upon the foundation of the apostles and prophets, with Christ Jesus himself as the capstone. Through him the whole structure is held together and grows into a temple sacred in the Lord; in him you also are being built together into a dwelling place of God in the Spirit. (Eph. 2:19–22)

Paul indicates to us that the church we belong to is a dwelling place of God who is CHESED' its capstone is none other than Jesus Christ who is an embodiment of God's CHESED it is built upon the foundation of the apostles and prophets who were the aftermath effect of resurrected CHESED and this is why those of us who are gathered in this structure are no more strangers to each other; we are fellow citizens along with all holy members who are again blossomed out of the resurrected CHESED'.

Therefore with Pope Francis, we can shout out to the universe that our church is nothing but the CHESED home. We should never deny what we profess in our creed about the characteristics of the church: "I believe in one, holy, Catholic and apostolic Church." We should also never forget all that those four qualifications of the church can be contained in the term "mercy home." The oneness and unity of the church, its holiness and apostolic roots all flow out of the mercy home, as well as they are targeted to testify its primary purpose. There is only one way to attest that the church we live in is God's dwelling place. As John writes in his book of Revelation (21:1-5) about a loud voice he heard from the heavenly throne, the humans must witness tangibly the following: (1) The presence of God inside the church intimately connected to them; (2) people's tears are wiped from their eyes; and (3) there is among them no more death or mourning, wailing, or pain.

In the Bible, we come across many expressions exuberantly portraying the nature and mission of the church, such as the Bride of Christ, the Body of Christ, and so on. Since the church is nothing but the personification of its gathered members, we also can ascertain that every Christian is the Bride of Christ and a member in that Body. In the same vein, when the church is esteemed as the structure of the dwelling of God in this world, with Peter, we can proudly aver we are the living stones built in it like Jesus Christ (1 Pet. 2:4-5).

Church Is the Ark of God's **CHESED**

In order to expound the great mystery of the church, all church fathers and holy men and women of God have been employing many scriptural symbols and inspirational metaphors such as "Edifice of God," "Dwelling Place of God," "Holy Temple," "Holy City," "Body of Christ," "Bride of Jesus," "Mother of God's People," "Sheepfold of the Good Shepherd," and "Kingdom of God," and so on. Some preachers and writers like me glorify the unique role of the church on earth as "the Ark of the Covenant."

The relentless desire of God to be in covenantal relationship with humanity clearly comes forth in one of the most ancient and shocking events narrated in the OT. It centers on Noah's Ark around which a covenantal deal made between God and Noah (ref. Genesis chapters 6 through 9). As the holy Creator found "how worst the wickedness of human beings was on earth, and how every desire that their heart conceived was always nothing but evil," his graceful heart was broken. He decided to punish them, except for Noah, the only human who found favor with God because he was a righteous man and blameless. Bible underlines that Noah was bestowed a grace of even walking with God. This amicable relationship between the two, founded on CHESED became the base of the mutual covenant they made with each other. Mutual CHESED of the two exchanged their agreement: God guaranteed Noah that he would be spared while the entire human race would be destroyed by deluge; on the part of Noah, he guaranteed God that he would comply with whatever God had commanded him to do in building a huge ark and filling it with all of God's creatures—two of every kind and also guaranteed of their safety and security.

After the deluge event, God and Noah met together at a thanksgiving ritual together with family members; once again we see their covenant being renewed but with some distinction. While the first phase of their covenant was personal, at this moment God made Noah as the representative of the entire human race and renewed his covenant of never destroying the humanity again. For this promise of God, Noah and the rainbow were the eyewitnesses. In this aspect, we can call the church as the Ark of Noah, which is first and foremost the symbol of the New Covenant God made with Jesus to redeem all humans who are entering the ark.

In order to live a life of peace and joy in the midst of problems and temptations and to win our life's battle, each one of us has to try to find an abode of safety and security, of power and ammunitions, and of protection and cure. Indeed we try to choose the arks according to our whims and fancies. Many of us choose to join a group of our own as a safety network, comfort zone, quarantine, and rehabilitation center or as our smokehouses. They name it as tribe, caste, race, color, and cult. Some others choose a comfort zone of their own as nightclub or country club. Others choose to hide themselves in their own bedroom or sleep tight on their couches. Many of us use our peer groups as their ark of comfort zone. Many try to escape or to take it easy in this struggle by adhering to alcoholism, drug addiction, gambling, and so on. Even some make recourse to suicide, death.

In all these human attempts, we find certain flaws of inconsistencies and incapacity. Many times these arks add more harm and are injurious to our security and safety. In this precarious situation, many of us consider religion to be a suitable comfort zone. And that is what Karl Marx hinted at: "Religion is the opium of people." That way of viewing religion is not in the Good Book or in any of the traditions of the church. Yes, church is to be esteemed as the Ark of the Covenant. But on what basis?

Every Disciple Is the Ark of **CHESED**

The ark built by Noah at the advice of God and the ark Peter refers to in his letter (1 Pet. 3:18–22) and the "Kingdom of God" (Mark 1:15) Jesus preached answer our quest. They are the symbols of the Ark of the Covenant established by God for us to enter in and dwell happily and safely thereafter. As we see God renew and confirm his covenant with and through Noah, Peter claims that the church is a realm where through baptism God and humans make their covenantal treaty: "Baptism is not a removal of dirt from the body but an appeal to God for a clear conscience, through the resurrection of Jesus Christ, who has gone into heaven and is at the right hand of God, with angels, authorities, and powers subject to him." In other words, through baptism, the church members have entered into God's covenant; they have said OK to his loving call and started living a life of contract with Him. The same was true in the life of Jesus. After forty days of his life and solitude in the wilderness with God, Jesus accepted fully his Father's covenant as the kingdom and proclaimed it to us, saying, "This is the time of fulfillment. The kingdom of God is at hand. Repent, and believe in the gospel."

When Jesus ascertained that the Kingdom of God is at hand, within you and in the midst of you, he pointed out that surely the Kingdom is not of this world; rather it is a spiritual realm where God and humans meet together in the spirit of CHESED. God's kingdom that Jesus spoke of means a real life or a way of life that contains justice, love, peace; it is a kingdom of truth and life, a kingdom of holiness and grace. God has established this kingdom from the beginning of the universe and therefore it is eternal and universal. And it is on his eternal covenant of love which he made with Noah and reiterated to Abraham and his posterity till this day in Jesus. Jesus points out that such kingdom is now here at our door.

Therefore, this spiritual kingdom can be an inner sanctuary of human spirit or it can be called human conscience, and even as Paul and Peter assert, every human person is the temple of the Holy Spirit. This is the basics of clear view on the church, which only exists as the sign of God's CHESED and simultaneously visibly embedded in the CHESED fellowship of humans. In effect, the church can be called the Ark of the Covenant. If the base of mutual spiritual covenant is damaged by either of the party, there is no Ark effect at all.

Undoubtedly, the primary-party God will never be unfaithful to his covenant; the only suspicion is about the humans who may affiliate themselves into the external Ark of the Covenant but most of the time fake to be so in their spirit. It is a historical and biblical fact that God have never been violating or going against his covenantal CHESED. It is humans who have been losing track of their promises and not responding to God's call of justice, mercy, and faithfulness. For such pretenders, the Holy Ark will in no way become a magic comfort zone of safety and security in their troubles. There were times in the church history when many converts entered into the church and were baptized in order to protect their identity, to find safety and security from the cruel kings, emperors, and unjust regimes. It is true that according to the scriptures, the church, founded by Jesus, is not just any human system like a government or any other social network. If anyone wants to encounter the genuine comfort and joy inside the church, first and foremost they must be fully present inside the spiritual ark of CHESED. As a result, when such like-minded and CHESED-oriented individuals come together, the church is present—even "two or three gathered in his Name."

The following is a story told by Joyce Myers on TV, which one of my friends narrated in his version: A ragged little boy was walking alone in a shopping mall with shoes tattered, so his feet made contact with the floor tile with each step. Presently, a generous Christian woman extended her hand, smiled, and said, "Would you like a nice new pair of shoes?" He smiled and followed her into a shoe store. The lady politely asked for a bowl of water and rag and tenderly cleaned his feet. Then socks were lovingly placed on his little feet; an extra pair was stuffed into his empty pants pocket. The nicest pair of shoes were slipped onto his tiny feet. The little boy by now was overwhelmed with joy, being so much excited that tears overflowed. He unhesitantly asked her, "Are you God's wife?"

If we take pride in claiming that every member of the Church is living stone with which God's CHESED Dwelling Place is built, and if we contend that each one of us is the Bride of Jesus, the resurrected CHESED, we are indebted to inspire our fellowmen by the same CHESED full of our compassionate, just, and faithful deeds. This would do the ripple effects in the hearts of humans around us to raise a valid question: Are you the Bride of Christ? Are you the Dwelling Place of God?

CHAPTER 14

·⊹✦▒▒▒▒▒▒▒▒▒▒▒▒▒▒▒▒◆▒▒▒▒▒▒▒▒▒▒▒▒▒▒▒✦⊹·

The Refreshed CHESED of Twenty-First-Century Church

The Greatest **CHESED** *Dream of the Bride*

A lmost all the churches agree with John and other Synoptic Gospel writers who refer to Christ as the Bridegroom (John 3:29; Mark 2:19; Matt. 9:15; Luke 5:34; and Matt. 25:1–13). These claims came out of the evangelists' inferences from the metaphoric OT calling of God as the Bridegroom of Israel. As the Father had been a covenant-committed Bridegroom to his people, so the Son too is by covenant related to his people as a Bridegroom. As a follow-up of this fact, the church traditionally upholds that Christ is the Bridegroom of the New Israel as the Father had been to the Old Israel. To augment this, upholding church fathers quote many references from the book of Revelation (Rev. 19:7; Rev. 21:2, 9, 10; and Rev. 22:17). In all these instances, John calls the church as the Bride of Christ or the Lamb's Bride. Paul's words in Ephesians 5:22–33 are also brought into this discussion as he compares the union of a husband and a wife to that of Christ and the church. Plus, it is befitting to hold this claim for the natural metaphorical reason that a bridegroom must have a bride. For instance, when it is said by Matthew that the virgins were waiting for the Bridegroom's arrival at midnight, we have to ask who would be those virgins but none other than the group of souls? That group should be the church.

Following Paul's assertion, the CHESED duty of the church does not stop with getting mercy from the Bridegroom; rather in a nonstop way over the centuries, she has been proclaiming and witnessing the Gospel of CHESED throughout the whole world both in words and actions. The Bride of Christ is both a visionary like John the Evangelist and a missionary like Paul, the great Apostle. John, in his book of Revelation, as we mentioned earlier in this book, fills his visions about what the Greatest Visionary Jesus Christ dreamed. The core of them is the dream of realizing "new heaven and new earth," where replacing the old order a new one should be emerged (Rev. 21:1-8). While the old order is overwhelmed with the unfaithful, the depraved, murderers, the unchaste, sorcerers, idol worshipers, and deceivers of every sort, this new order is to be based and wheeled on God's CHESED, namely, mercy, justice, and fidelity.

It is true, this sort of dream about a new order is the perennial quest of our human race in groaning, as Paul underlines in his letter (Rom. 8:18-27). In every age, the leaders and gurus of the people promised such new order and offered many strategies to establish and maintain it. However, their definition of this "new order" and the strategy of achieving it have been totally different from those of Jesus. All these leaders and gurus in their enlightenment and intelligence listed many strategies, tricks, norms, and mantras at realizing this new order of life; but most of their tips turned out to be either unproductive or completely wrong and perverted, in some cases pharisaical diplomatic self-centered means.

According to the faith of the Bride of Christ, being enlightened by both the Spirit and the Scriptures, her Bridegroom had proclaimed that his very purpose of being born in this world was to establish this new order, the kingdom of God, as he labeled it; and so he did it not only by his life, death, and resurrection but also when he sent his resurrected Spirit upon his disciples. From that onward, the reign of life has begun and the tyranny of death is ended. A new birth has taken place, a new life has come, a new order of existence has appeared, and our very nature has been transformed! This birth is not brought about by human generation, by the will of man, or by the desire of the flesh, but by God. Faith is the womb that conceives this new life, baptism the rebirth by which it is brought forth into the light of day. The church is its nurse, her teachings are its milk, the bread from heaven is its food. It is brought to maturity by the practice of virtue; it is wedded to wisdom; it gives birth to hope. Its home is the kingdom; its rich inheritance the joys of paradise; its end, not death, but the blessed and everlasting life prepared for those who are worthy. Here below let us see some of the ingredients of church's dream.

Church Is a Multidimensional and Multipurpose Structure

The Bible and Catholic tradition have various images for describing the essence of the church. Many years back, Cardinal Ivory Dulles, SJ, beautifully and very scripturally and traditionally described the church's identity in five portrayals: Institution, Mystical Body, Communion, Herald of God's word, Servant, and Sacrament. Going through various phases and efforts, the church's understanding about her own nature and identity, and emphasizing the unique internal and external reality of the church, Cardinal Dulles consolidated into these five concepts. Many theologians and surely church councils deliberated in many centuries the twofold dimension of the church as universal and local, visionary and missionary, already and not yet, holy and sinful, traditional and innovative, doctrinal and practical, authoritative and pastoral. Therefore, the endless theological debates are continued in theological and ecclesiological circles to come to a conclusion of the unique reality of the Church. However, I think it is Jesus's intention that his church must be a multidimensional and multipurpose structure in this world. This has to be so not only due to its rare-blend perennial nature of both divine and human elements, but also because of the Creator's brilliant will of ascertaining the beauty of his creation consisting in its unity in diversity.

Church Is Evangelization

Very relevantly, in every age, the Spirit of Jesus moved the church to accentuate one or two of its dimensions in the context of the church members and also the secular world losing the grip of those elements. For example, from the Middle Ages to the nineteenth century, as Cardinal Dulles wrote in the magazine *FIRST THINGS*, March

1996, Catholicism has put the accent on the corporate and traditional features of Christianity. The Catholic Church has been the church of organization, dogma, and sacraments. While always sponsoring missionary activity, the Catholic Church has relied chiefly on religious orders to perform this task. They were expected not so much to spread the Gospel as to plant the church in countries where it had as yet no roots. Thanks to the Spirit's movement, the II Vatican Council emphasized forcefully that every Christian has a responsibility to evangelize. Pope Paul VI followed this up by composing his great apostolic exhortation, "Evangelization in the Modern World," 1975, where he categorically stated that the deepest identity of the church is *evangelization*, which means the church exists in order to evangelize.

In the footsteps of Pope Paul VI, his successors, especially John Paul II, took it very seriously and was daring enough to call himself "a pilgrim pope of evangelization." He declared, while he visited Mexico in 1983, that God calls the church in the New Millennium to commit all her energies to a new evangelization. He ascertained, more urgent than ever, that the church must demonstrate the importance of the Christian message for all the peoples of the world and to revitalize Christian faith in parts of the world where it has become feeble or inert. Such contextual emphasis did not in any way belittle other elements and dimensions of the church; it never lost sight of the doctrine of "salvation by faith alone," but more relentlessly, it brought home to believers that we should strive to renew the entire life of the church and of society through the leaven of the Gospel. It did not separate word from sacraments, or faith from works, or personal morality from social action; the only "evangelization effect" proposed was a regeneration of the entire community of believers in the light of the Gospel and to transform the larger secular society in the image of the kingdom of God.

The Unforgettable Paradigm Shift

The divine Bridegroom has been always a surprise to his Bride. During the second decade of the twenty-first century, he appeared again in the personality of Pope Francis. Jesus decided once and for all through the fragile, sickly, but faith-filled and Spirit-filled pope to make a thorough shakeup and shapeup and cleanup in his church. He made him to move on the New Evangelization Road his predecessors took but with difference. As we pointed out, it was the need of this new century in which so many abuses and in fights perfusedly contaminated and disfigured the beautiful holiness of the Bride; plus the technologically and scientifically and even economically developed modern world has drifted away from the CHESED of God's plan for his creation.

The Second Vatican Council renewed that understanding and presented the church as the messianic people of God (Lumen Gentium, 9–12). While so many well-read people in different continents interpreted this view with reservations, in South America, the impulse of the council was eagerly seized upon and further developed into the theology of the people. When the Argentine cardinal Bergoglio was elected as Pope Francis, he came into the mainstream of the church freshly bringing with him this ecclesiology of the people of God with concrete life.

In his encyclical *Evangelii gaudium*, he splendidly proclaimed the true identity and essence of today's church. In his speech to the bishops of Brazil in Rio de Janeiro, he said very clearly what he meant by such a conversion:

> I would like to remind you that "pastoral care" is nothing other than the exercise of the church's motherhood. She gives birth, breastfeeds, lets grow, corrects, nourishes, leads by the hand . . . . There is need therefore for a church that is capable of rediscovering the womb of mercy. Without mercy it is scarcely possible today to penetrate into a world of the "injured," who need understanding, forgiveness, and love. (Quoted by Cardinal Walter Kasper in his article "How Pope Francis Sees the Church," *Commonweal*, March 2015.)

Church Is Merciful Mother

Pope Francis's main thrust in his pontificate has been not making the church populist or papalist; rather it must be a home of CHESED, God's mercy. He believes firmly that the church and her salvific undertakings are rooted in the CHESED of the Trinity. Hence, the church gets every bit of her glory, dignity, and power only from the primacy of grace. Therefore, he insists, as Cardinal Kasper points out, "the church must be the place of renegotiated mercy, where all can feel themselves welcomed and loved, where they experience pardon and can feel encouraged to live according to the good life of the Gospel."

In that same spirit of CHESED, Pope Francis wanted the church to behave as a "merciful mother" regarding administering sacraments with an open heart for all. He has many times reiterated his favorite HESED litany: "The Church should be an open house with open door." He too adds that it must be like a field hospital to heal the wounded and the dying. This idea of mercy is not something new and an off-the-cuff statement from the pope. History tells us that against the rigorism of Novatian, Cyprian supported the cause of clemency and mercy toward the lapsed Christians. The church, though many times some of her leaders overemphasized publicly her secondary roles, never lost her focus on her primary role being a "merciful mother." Privately so, many priests, nuns, and laity have been strenuously striving to maintain and witness to the primary role of the church. Here I am reminded of one of my Tamil multistage dramas I directed and staged with my theater troupe in many churches in South India. It was about the life and mission of Frederick Ozannam, the founder of Vincent De Paul Society. I gave it a striking name: *Mathame Theruvukku Vaa* (O Religion! Come out to the streets!) That was the manifesto of Ozannam French Catholic layman for all his merciful deeds he and his friends did. Till this day in all parts of the Catholic church, his Vincent De Paul Society continues relentlessly his dream of CHESED in action.

Church Is **CHESED** Home

Thanks to the Spirit of Jesus, today, Pope Francis shouts out loudly, visibly and uncompromisingly, this remarkable role of the church in this postmodern age, which is populated with millions of humans that are so individualistic, provincial, unjust, and earthly that they have become cold and frozen and blindfolded to billions of people in their own neighborhoods undergoing maladies of poverty, sickness, inequality, hatred, etc. At this milieu, Pope Francis proclaims day in and day out that we need a church that is bruised, hurting, and dirty because it has been out on the streets rather than a church remaining shuttered within its structures while outside a starving multitude waits.

The pope's vision of the church was already spelled out by him lucidly during the preconclave period: "The church should not be focused on itself; it ought not be a church that is narcissistically in love with itself, that revolves around itself. A self-involved human being is a sick human being; a self-involved church is a sick church" (EG, 43). Therefore, he insisted we must come out of the hackneyed air of a church that is self-involved—suffering from its own condition, bemoaning or celebrating itself. The global family joyfully recognized the new pope's mind-set. He longs to see our church to be an open house, a father's house in which there is a place for everyone with their difficulties. He has very beautifully put every element in the church in the right perspective as the Master dreamed of. It is to make the church a CHESED home, where according to the pope's new paradigm, we would be experiencing and exercising a "mysticism of coexistence and encounter," of embracing and supporting one another, of participating in a caravan of solidarity, in a sacred pilgrimage; a mystical and contemplative fraternity, which "knows how to see the sacred grandeur of our neighbor, of finding God in every human being" (EG, 92).

CHAPTER 15

Primary CHESED Duty of the Church

Under the influence and inspiration of the CHESED of Jesus's Spirit, from its beginning, the church, as the Bride of Christ, esteemed the rite of imploring God's mercy as her primary duty. The CHESED of God in Jesus demands from the Bride the same kind of mercy, justice, and fidelity. Discussing that the genuine relationship to be existing between husbands and wives must be like that of between Jesus and the church, Paul remarkably describes this bond between the Divine Bridegroom and his Church:

> As the church is subordinate to Christ . . . even as Christ loved the church and handed himself over for her to sanctify her, cleansing her by the bath of water with the word, that he might present to himself the church in splendor, without spot or wrinkle or any such thing, that she might be holy and without blemish." (Eph. 5:24–27)

Church history attests that the church, due to her weakness, has been unfaithful many times toward her

Bridegroom. Being fully conscious of her sinfulness, therefore, she has included the penitential rite in all her liturgical practices. In a special way, she does this in her regular Masses. At the start of the Mass, we are directed to plead the mercy from heaven reciting three times "Kyrie Eleison," ending with the priest saying, "May almighty God have mercy on us." In the hymn of "Gloria" again, we sing twice to Jesus, the HESED enfleshed, requesting him to "have mercy on us." The celebrant makes frequent references to the church's appeal for mercy in all Eucharistic Prayers (EP): "in your abundant mercies" (EP-I); "Have mercy on us all" (EP-II); "in your compassion, O merciful Father" (EP-III); inserting "for you came in mercy to the aid of all" in the preface; and "Grant in your loving kindness" and "Grant, O merciful Father" (EP-IV). In the Communion rite, the celebrant recites in the extension prayer to our Father, "Lord, by the help of your mercy." Before approaching the Table of the Lord for Communion, the congregation is asked again to recite to the Lamb of God, "Have mercy on us."

Besides being approved by the Bridegroom, she has developed a religious scheme administering the seven sacraments to the members. In every sacramental form, we can find frequent references to her need of mercy from the Divine; plus three of those sacraments—baptism, reconciliation, and anointing of the sick—directly concerned with conferring God's mercy through the empowerment she has been bestowed with by her Bridegroom.

CHESED *Way Is the Only Way*

In the previous chapter, we discussed about the Bridegroom's one and only way to become full-fledged members in that new order of life. That is to observe the CHESED as he has successfully accomplished: "Love one another as I have loved you." His Bride well understood what her Bridegroom was proposing to her and tries her best to do so meticulously.

Let us delve into the spirit of Jesus behind his new commandment of love. In many religions, we have the similar commandment that urges people to love their neighbors as themselves. This is based on the golden rule ever present in any civilized societies that expects citizens to "do unto others what you have them do unto you." This indicates the justice part of Hesed ordering us to "give respect and get respect"; it's a mutual give-and-take policy for preserving the beauty and glory of any civilization. But Jesus's command goes up not just one step but so many steps ahead and demands from us to love one another not only as ourselves but as he has loved us. How does he want us to love one another as he does? It is simply CHESED the rare blend of mercy, justice, and faithfulness. Let me explain this in the scriptural and ecclesiological thoughts.

CHESED *of the Bride Is Love in Agape-Style*

The word *agape* means the "unlimited, pure love of God." Jesus's human love was fully centered on God and his love. His Father God is Love itself. The Lord, whom we worship, is "gracious and merciful, slow to anger and of great kindness"; he is "good to all and compassionate toward all his works"; "he so loved us that he sent his only begotten Son to us." In plain words, our God is faithful in his love eternally. The same thing was true in Jesus's life. On his part, he reciprocates his love for his Father faithfully by obeying his will even if that will lead him to an ignominious death on the cross so that his Father's design could be accomplished. In the new order, he established that God and his love is central and the basis as well: God's dwelling is with the human race. Whoever tries to enter into this dwelling of CHESED will be his people; he himself will always be with them as their God; he will wipe every tear from their eyes.

This means that in this new order, the risen Lord is ever present among humans as Emmanuel, God with us. In him, the world and heaven, the flesh and the spirit, the weak and the strong, the sinners and the righteous, the pagans and the chosen ones are bonded together, not just nominally related together, not merely by justice, but integrated together by their fidelity to the CHESED of God. It's very clear that the ultimate goal of the risen Lord's active presence is nothing but to realize one day "One world and under One God," "One flock under one Shepherd." In this new order, our human love affair in all its dimensions must start from God's love, proceed in God's love, and end with God's love as our ultimate goal. This is what we mean by agape-styled love of the Bride.

SECTION V

The CHESED Deeds of the Blessed

Psalm 103:8

*Hashem is rachum and channun, slow to
anger, and plenteous in* **chesed**.

—OJB

*Merciful and gracious is the LORD, slow
to anger, abounding in* **mercy**.

—NABRE

After knowing the full meaning of the term mercy as part of CHESED, which is the character and behavior of God and of his Son Jesus Christ and of the Church, the Bride of Jesus, let us now discuss about how we as individuals live our Christian life based on the same CHESED.

There are three ways of performing an act of mercy: the merciful word, by forgiving and by comforting; secondly, if you can offer no word, then by praying—that too is mercy; and thirdly, deeds of mercy. And when the Last Day comes, we shall be judged from this, and on this basis we shall receive the eternal verdict. (Saint Faustina)

CHAPTER 16

The Spirit behind Our Merciful Acts

By biblical revelation, as we underscored in the first chapter, CHESED should be viewed as mutual and reciprocal interaction of the Divine and the human. In the second chapter, we elaborately discussed about the CHESED actions of God toward humans. The third chapter contained all the CHESED undertakings accomplished in the universal church. Now our attention is focused on how every follower of Christ, as a private or personal church, should demonstrate hesed to the Almighty.

The church is nothing but a realm or a domain where both God and Jesus's followers come together. Traditionally, we have heard that "where the bishop is, there is the Church." It may be right for recognizing the church's external dimension. But regarding its internal identity, its existence has to be witnessed in every member's spiritual relations with their Master, the Bridegroom, and the CHESED enfleshed. Every member in the church is not only the living stones with which the universal church is built but also is considered as the individual Dwelling of God, Temple of the Holy

Spirit, and the Branch and Stem of the Divine Vine. Significantly, each member in the Body of Christ can be called the "personal church"; when individual churches form a family, it is called the "domestic church," and when these domestic churches gather together under a bishop, they make the "local church."

Before we go into the list of the merciful acts of the "blessed," let us talk over the spirit behind those acts in order to become the sources of the promised "blessedness." As our Master said, "a good person out of the store of goodness in his heart produces good, but an evil person out of a store of evil produces evil; for from the fullness of the heart the mouth speaks" (Luke 6:45). He too pointed out how our interior disposition can influence our exterior actions: "The lamp of the body is the eye. If your eye is sound, your whole body will be filled with light; but if your eye is bad, your whole body will be in darkness. And if the light in you is darkness, how great will the darkness be" (Matt. 6:22–23).

All the NT writers were ever attuned to what God's Spirit said through his messengers in the past who proclaimed insistently that the primary source of blessedness for humans is nothing but the CHESED-based attitude:

> Blessed are those who trust in the LORD; the LORD will be their trust. They are like a tree planted beside the waters that stretches out its roots to the stream: It does not fear heat when it comes, its leaves stay green; in the year of drought it shows no distress, but still produces fruit. (Jer. 17:7–8)

> Blessed the one whose help is the God of
> Jacob, whose hope is in the LORD, his
> God, the maker of heaven and earth, the
> seas and all that is in them, who keeps faith
> forever, secures justice for the oppressed, who
> gives bread to the hungry. The LORD sets
> prisoners free; the LORD gives sight to the
> blind. The LORD raises up those who are
> bowed down; the LORD loves the righteous.
> The LORD protects the resident alien, comes
> to the aid of the orphan and the widow, but
> thwarts the way of the wicked. (Ps. 146:5–9)

Undoubtedly, the words of Jesus, which are quoted in the Gospels, are the continued assertion of CHESED attitude of blessedness for humans. Therefore, it is good to know what sort of attitude we should possess as we accomplish our merciful acts. This inner outlook can be called our "interior disposition," "inner spirit," or our "mind-setup."

Being Merciful as Our God

Before we list out the five CHESED-oriented actions each one of us should perform in this world, we should be very clear about how those actions are to be accomplished so that we can covet their ultimate end results. For this, we need not go anywhere in search. Our Master Jesus has proposed the *how* of it very beautifully. He said, "Be merciful as your heavenly Father is merciful." In the second section, we emphasized that God's CHESED is a rare blend of justice, mercy, and fidelity. We also said that in all of God's deeds, all these three are concomitantly found. Therefore, if we desire to be merciful as our heavenly Father is, all our deeds of mercy also must be melded with justice and fidelity.

To imitate God in doing merciful acts, first, our mercy must be blended with justice. Justice is something that should be practiced along with mercy and faithfulness. They are not mutually exclusive as we observe in God. This is what the Almighty expects us to do: "You have been told, O mortal, what is good, and what the LORD requires of you: Only to do justice and to love goodness, and to walk humbly with your God" (Mic. 6:8). This way of acting justly and being merciful as well is possible, as God insists, when we walk humbly with him. We are supposed to administer justice with a heart of mercy. Jesus exhorted the same to his disciples as he expounded the most important matters of the law: "Justice, mercy and faithfulness" (Matt. 23:23).

Second, our mercy should be based on justice but performed in faithfulness, which is simply a restful but resourceful settlement in God's will. Every act we do in mercy is to be steadfast, meaning that it begins, proceeds, and ends with a firm and unwavering attitude in purpose and loyalty to the Creator. That is why King David cries aloud to God not to take away the Holy Spirit but begs to refresh it, referring to his steadfast spirit:

> Clean heart create for me, God; renew within me a steadfast spirit. Do not drive me from before your face, nor take from me your holy spirit. Restore to me the gladness of your salvation; uphold me with a willing spirit. (Ps. 51:12–14)

Tobit, being a God-fearing dad, exhorts his son at the sunset of his life:

> Through all your days, son, keep the Lord in mind, and do not seek to sin or to transgress the commandments. Perform righteous deeds all the days of your life, and do not tread the paths of wickedness. For those who act with fidelity, all who practice righteousness, will prosper in their affairs. (Tobit 4:5–6)

The above-noted way of imitating God in his mercy is easier to say than doing. Hence, Jesus and his apostles left behind to the church and her members their own teachings and examples for how humans can accomplish this dream. I want to remind the readers about the historical beginning of the church's most witnessing acts of mercy through deacons. In Acts 6:1-10, we read about a critical situation at the early church community in Jerusalem. As so many new people of different races become disciples of Jesus, and most of them were widows and the needy, the apostles experienced a hard time of coping with fulfilling her Master's desire of serving the people by preaching, praying, and performing mercy deeds. Hence, the Spirit of the Lord quickly enlightened the apostles in solving simultaneously these spiritual, religious, and social problems. Luke tells us what the apostles addressed to their community: "It is not right for us to neglect the word of God to serve at table." And they placed before them their recommendation, which has become the norm of the church till this day.

What they did was a most admirable thing. They selected seven men from the community and entrusted to them the ministry of carrying out merciful deeds while they kept the ministries of praying, teaching, and preaching. Those chosen seven then were called "the deacons" (1 Tim.). The word *deacon*, derived from the Greek word *diákonos*, meaning "servant," "waiting man," "minister," or "messenger." In other words, they would perform the role of the agents of Jesus primarily in handing out food, water, dress, shelter, etc.

The surprising factor in this event of choosing proper persons for serving the poor and the needy was that deacons, like Stephan, were indeed filled with grace and power, and besides their regular charitable services, they worked signs and wonders among the people and amazingly defended their faith in Jesus through their powerful words. On this, Luke says that in their apologetic teaching, their opponents "could not withstand their wisdom and the spirit with which they spoke" (Acts 6:8–10).

The most relevant point in our discussion in this chapter is the requirements needed for becoming a deacon of serving the needy and the poor. The apostles, as they appointed the first group of deacons, ministers of charities, exhorted their community to choose "reputable men, filled with the Spirit and wisdom" (Acts 6:3). And Paul, in keeping with the admonitions and customs of the apostles, portrayed clearly the qualities proper to deacons who primarily do merciful acts.

> Deacons must be dignified, not deceitful, not addicted to drink, not greedy for sordid gain, holding fast to the mystery of the faith with a clear conscience. Moreover, they should be tested first; then, if there is nothing against

them, let them serve as deacons. (1 Tim.
3:8–10)

The reason why I included the adverb *primarily* into
the deacons' roles is as Luke noted about the fact that
even the first group of deacons carried out some other
roles as Jesus's disciples, as it needed, in the course of
church history, the deacons who are ordained in mainline
churches as well as laypeople who are honored as deacons
in other denominations, continue to undertake with the
primary role of mercy deeds, the ministry of serving the
worship, in pastoral care and even on administrative
committees.

This NT scriptural and historical reflection about the
creation of the deaconate in the church adds fuel to our
discussion on the spirit and motivation of "the merciful"
living today who are bound not only to witness Jesus in
words and in power but also through merciful deeds.

Attitude of Beatitudes

Yes, the merciful must possess the spirit Jesus codifies
in his nine beatitudes (Matt. 5:3–12). In my introduction
to this book, I explained how Jesus's beatitudes are
positioned in Matthew's Gospel as a preface to all that
has been written about Jesus and his Gospel. Here I want
to highlight the predominant place given to the beatitude
of mercy in those beatitudes. As one preacher described,
it takes the central position among all beatitudes. While
the first four beatitudes deal with the basic attitudes of
the disciples Jesus dreamed about (verses 3–6) and the last
four cover their outward behavior (verses 8–11), the fifth

beatitude that proclaims the blessedness of being merciful stands in the middle! Very interesting, isn't?

This suggests that being merciful should be the core duty and responsibility of the disciples; plus the practice of mercy must not only originate from a heart that is poor, broken, contrite, and meek, but also adorned by purity, peace, righteousness, and closeness to Jesus. Jesus first possessed these attitudes in all of his undertakings as a Jew of Nazareth. Many may reject his Gospel of beatitudes as a utopian and undoable ideal, and we too agree with them in one way. Everything he put forth to us as a means of blessedness carries with it hardship of discipline. When he was perplexed in this regard, he encouraged them by saying, "What is impossible for human beings is possible for God" (Luke 18:27). All committed disciples of Jesus know that he came to us, besides for teaching us the Way of Life, for making us what he taught we should be. His redemptive role is centered on putting into us the attitudes that ruled his own life. Paul longed for these attitudes and so he directed us also to uphold them. He excellently summed up the entire Gospel of beatitudes in one single attitude. Have among yourselves the same attitude that is also yours in Christ Jesus (Phil. 2:5).

Spirit of Anawim

In scriptural terms, we can name this "single attitude" as the spirit of Anawim. *Anawim* is a Hebrew term meaning the needy and empty spirit. It is used frequently in the Bible, especially the Psalms; most importantly, it is the basis for Jesus's statement "Blessed are the poor." Anawim biblically refers to the vulnerable, the marginalized, and socioeconomically oppressed, those of lowly status without earthly power. It indicates not only the pathetic social status of those unfortunate humans but also concurrently implies their internal disposition of being dependent totally on God for whatever they owned even it would be like "the widow's mite." Sr. Joan L. Roccasalvo CSJ well portrayed about the Anawim of our time in one of her blogs in 2012: "Apparently, children, saints, and fools are the only ones who can be admired as anawim. And now the hurricane victims."

In this perspective, Paul proclaimed his belief that Jesus was number one Anawim in the kingdom of God (Phil. 2:6-7). In the light of NT books, we discover that the spirit of anawim in Jesus was comprised of three elements. Describing the incarnation of Christ, Paul's first emphasis was Christ's kenosis: "He emptied himself." Gospel writers proved this kenosis as telling us the words of Jesus: "Foxes have dens and birds of the sky have nests, but the Son of Man has nowhere to rest his head" (Luke 9:58). His spirit of anawim included certainly the most crucial dimension in that spirit, namely, his total dependence to his Father:

He said I and Father are one. (John 10:30)

But he also reiterated, by myself I can do nothing. (John 5:30)

When you lift up the Son of Man, then you will realize that I AM, and that I do nothing on my own, but I say only what the Father taught me. The one who sent me is with me.

> He has not left me alone, because I always do
> what is pleasing to him. (John 8:28–29)

Besides, Jesus was meticulously fulfilling God's will as his food:

> My food is to do the will of the one who sent
> me and to finish his work. (John 4:34)

> I came down from heaven not to do my own
> will but the will of the one who sent me.
> (John 6:38)

From his conception till his last breath, his only preoccupation was to accomplish God's will, not simply to go with the flow but even swim against the current. As his first word was "Behold, I come to do your will" (Heb. 10:7), so was his final hours' desire: "Father, if you are willing, take this cup away from me; still, not my will but yours be done" (Luke 22:42).

The third element found in Jesus's anawim spirit was what he did with his kenosis. Paul underlines this fact: "For you know the gracious act of our Lord Jesus Christ, that for your sake he became poor although he was rich, so that by his poverty you might become rich" (2 Cor. 8:9). In other words, Jesus became anawim out of his CHESED love (agape) to deliver humanity from death to life, from poverty to prosperity.

Jesus demanded from his disciples the same three-dimensional spirit of anawim if they prefer to reap the genuine heavenly results out of their discipleship of mercy, justice, and faithfulness. That is why when he pronounced that the merciful are the blessed, he first demanded such spirit of poverty, meekness, brokenness, purity, and righteousness, which are constituents of anawim spirit. Whoever do the works of mercy with this spirit, they will never be tired of such works, never be offended by ingratitude of beneficiaries, always being ready to break the ice in human relationship, countless times forgiving our sinful and ignorant neighbors, courageously moving forward to go beyond the lethargy, stillness, and exploring new vistas by constant but CHESED-oriented paradigm shift.

Disposition of Remnant

The remnant mentioned in the OT are the chosen people, like Noah's family, whom the Lord saved from social and political and natural calamities and preserved them safe and sound. He fulfilled his promise as foretold through prophets: "I will leave as a remnant in your midst a people humble and lowly, who shall take refuge in the name of the LORD, the remnant of Israel" (Zeph. 3:12). Through Prophet Ezekiel, God described how he would be creating a renewed generation from his people in a breathtaking way:

> I will show the holiness of my great name, desecrated among the nations, in whose midst you desecrated it. Then the nations shall know that I am the LORD when through you I show my holiness before their very eyes. I will take you away from among the nations, gather you from all the lands, and bring you back to your own soil. I will sprinkle clean

> water over you to make you clean; from all
> your impurities and from all your idols I will
> cleanse you. I will give you a new heart, and a
> new spirit I will put within you. I will remove
> the heart of stone from your flesh and give
> you a heart of flesh. I will put my spirit within
> you so that you walk in my statutes, observe
> my ordinances, and keep them. You will live
> in the land I gave to your ancestors; you will
> be my people, and I will be your God. (Ez.
> 36:23–28)

The remnants were those people whom God liberated in marvelous means from their exilic life, from their slavery and from all their political and social maladies; above all, by sending his Son to humanity, he offered them spiritual liberation from sins. All who are saved by Jesus's cross are known as the remnant. Peter portrays them as a chosen race, a royal priesthood, a holy nation, a people of his own so that you may announce the praises of him who called you out of darkness into his wonderful light (1 Pet. 2:9).

In history, we observe God, though not one-sided, acting always on his spirit of love and dealing with every one of his people in accordance with each one's free will and capability. In relationship with God, many go round and round at the surface while some get closer and closer, higher and higher, and deeper and deeper in their rapport with him. In the eyes of Jesus, the remnant are those of his followers who were cleansed by his Blood and through his grace pledge and live up to his beatitudes. He implied mainly those remnants that survive and stay on the side of God in the continued war going on between the Good and the Evil, between God and the Satan.

Once, I visited a dying person in a nursing home. He had several sons and daughters of whom only one daughter was present there at his deathbed. I asked her about other family members. She stood in tears. After her mother's death, as I heard from her, she was the only one who stayed with her father in his ailment and medical treatment. Though other relatives were living in the same town, they didn't care for this old man. As we all imagine, her dad left all his property and savings in his will for this loving daughter. He honored her as the only remnant worthy of his love. She was finally blessed and rewarded by him for what she was.

Even though the good Lord showers his blessings on his humans unconditionally and with no strings attached, I feel that God's choice of people as his remnants is very much connected to justice, an intrinsic part of his CHESED. He won't throw his pearls to the swine nor will he give holy things to dogs. As Jesus said, in God's realm, many are called but few are chosen. Out of his justice, freedom, and truth, God cannot but make his choices regarding humans on the basis of humans' freedom and capacity. Hence his kindhearted gesture of saving and securing certain people in history is totally for one purpose—of witnessing to the CHESED-based covenant both he and his people made before and after he performed such miraculous deeds.

Before discussing about the remnant, Prophet Zephaniah spells out who would those be who will find favor with God: "Seek the LORD, all you humble of the land, who have observed his law; Seek justice, seek humility; Perhaps you will be sheltered on the day of the

LORD's anger" (Zeph. 2:3). He too, after mentioning about the amazing "remnant position" offered by God, cautions the remnant on how to preserve that position till the end: "They shall do no wrong and speak no lies; nor shall there be found in their mouths a deceitful tongue; they shall pasture and lie down with none to disturb them" (Zeph. 3:13).

This is what Jesus expected from his remnant. His list of beatitudes in the Gospel covers a compendium of all that is said about the remnant of God. In Jesus's mind, the true remnants of God are those who are poor in spirit, those who mourn, those who are meek, those who hunger and thirst for righteousness, those who are merciful, those who are clean of heart, those who are peacemakers, and those who are persecuted for the sake of righteousness. Paul, the favorite Apostle of Jesus, expands his Master's view on the spirit of the remnant by saying, "These people are the foolish of the world; the weak of the world; the lowly and despised of the world; and they are those who count for nothing" (1 Cor. 1:26–28).

There is one more element in the spirit of the remnant. They are, at the gratuitousness of God, rescued and protected by him in order, as Paul declares, to shame the wise, to shame the strong, and to reduce to nothing those who are something. In this connection, let us remember the canticle of Mary about the roles of God's remnants: "He has thrown down the rulers from their thrones but lifted up the lowly. The hungry he has filled with good things; the rich he has sent away empty" (Luke 1:46–53). Jesus profusely promises the blessed end of the remnant: The kingdom of heaven is theirs, they will be comforted, they will inherit the Land, they will be satisfied, they will be shown mercy, they will see God, they will be called children of God, and their reward will be great in heaven too.

Human **chesed** *Is Grace + Gratitude + Mercy*

When we perform some love deeds, we often hear from our Hispanic friends saying to us *muchas gracias*, meaning "thanks a lot." *Gracia* is from the Latin root *gratia*, which refers also to "grace." Now surprisingly to indicate "thank you," French people use the term *merci*, which also means "mercy." What I admire at this linguistic interlink usages is how the humans amalgamate *grace, gratitude*, and *mercy* in their day-today social life's rendezvous: Many of us still say the grace before meals to recognize that our food is a gift from God; as an expression of thanks, we write and say that we are grateful for someone's kindness, gratified by the good happenings; we congratulate when our friends are successful; we behave graciously in hosting friends; in the restaurants, we leave a gratuity for a pleasant service; in music composition, a composer may add grace notes to the score.

In this mind-blowing perspective, if we deeply go into the meaning of CHESED humans are covenantaly committed to, we discover those three elements—grace, gratitude, and mercy, being its constituents. We resolutely believe that our spiritual survival depends only on God's grace; we steadfastly feel grateful to him and faithfully reciprocate our thanks to him by performing merciful acts to our neighbors. Our covenantal promises to God and their fulfillment in our life is swirled around, as some theologians call, the immense "gratitude-filled consciousness" of God's active presence in our ordinary lives.

There is an intrinsic and natural flow between these CHESED constituents. As any gift that comes from God is a free gift, when humans receive it and feel they have received so, their hearts beat with a thank-you note. Consequently, we can boldly say that a grace would become an incomplete gift if it is not accompanied with gratitude. Plus, mere consciousness of the gift of grace and on account of it lisping to God some words like *deo gratias* or *muchas gracias* would not suffice to fulfill our CHESED to him. We must also alongside do the merciful deeds externally for God's needy people.

God the giver of gifts daily advertises to us about his free gift cards worth millions; there is nothing great compared to those gift cards. In the book of Isaiah, the Lord does this promotion of his free gift cards:

> All you who are thirsty, come to the water! You who have no money, come, buy grain and eat; Come, buy grain without money, wine and milk without cost! Why spend your money for what is not bread; your wages for what does not satisfy? Only listen to me, and you shall eat well, you shall delight in rich fare. Pay attention and come to me; listen, that you may have life. I will make with you an everlasting covenant, the steadfast loyalty promised to David. (Isa. 55:1-3)

These free gifts God promised prophetically are sumptuous meals and drinks of eternal godly life through his CHESED covenant he made with us in Jesus.

Whatever God gives is free gift, but it is not a cheap grace either. We cannot have a free ride or enjoy a freebie in God's kingdom. In order to get all the benefits from God, as any free gift card receiver is expected to do, we have to participate in the gift giver's demand; namely, with a sincere heart, we need to take part in his banquet of grace and mercy not only as his guests but also in his delegated place as hosts of serving his sumptuous food of joy, love, justice, and peace to everyone whom he chooses. He has done so much for us. Therefore, he expects us to be mindful of all those blessings. All the gifts are privileges that require responsible responses. "Without cost we have received; without cost we are to give." *Noblesse oblige*, that means "Privilege entails responsibility." God's blessings are like a huge shower pouring down from heaven and only those bowls and ponds that are left open receive them and be filled. Therefore with no anxiety or despair regarding the failures and rejection or ingratitude we experience from our beneficiaries, we should be steadfast in our stride of mercy.

In Order To Be the "Blessed"

All who dream of becoming "the blessed" must therefore be guzzled with the above-discussed—the attitude of beatitude, the spirit of anawim, and the disposition of the remnant. Very sadly, not all those who are present in the external kingdom of God, the social religious structure, are fit to be called the blessed. According to Saint Augustine, there are two dimensions of the church established by Jesus: One is the visible church and the other is an invisible church. All who are visibly, sacramentally baptized, registered, and practicing their faith externally make the visible church whereas those who have been spiritually, intrinsically, and intimately connected with God in Jesus, even if they are not visibly demonstrating their identity, are the ones who form the invisible reality of the church. Unfortunately, those of the first dimension, though they nominally belong to the church, compromise, misinterpret, justify, and liquidate the Gospel of Jesus and the will of God. They move around on the surface level of the church. What they practice is simply, as one author puts it, a "Christianity lite." On the contrary, the second group belonging to the invisible church, being named as the remnants of God, accept willingly Jesus's call to holiness as their life choice and lifestyle. They live a life described in today's readings. They can be in Christianity and in other sections of the society as well. These remnants remain inside the world as the yeast, as seed, as light, and as salt doing the work of the Lord. They are in the world but not of the world. They suffer and die, but they turn out to be the source of inspirations, aspirations to the humanity. They live as effective means and tools in the hands of God in fulfilling his plan of salvation.

My final comment on this subject is that all those who perform merciful deeds both inside and outside the church, as some sort of "philanthropic" good acts or out of a kind of platonic love-oriented, cannot be called the blessed. This is what Jesus instructed us. In order to produce solid (heavenly) results, by all means we should primarily abide within his spirit.

> Remain in me, as I remain in you . . .
> Whoever remains in me and I in him will

bear much fruit, because without me you can do nothing. Anyone who does not remain in me will be thrown out like a branch and wither; people will gather them and throw them into a fire and they will be burned. (John 15:4-6)

CHAPTER 17

Our CHESED Action 1: Ceaselessly Soliciting the Enduring Mercy of God

The Amazing but Costly Gift of Mercy

The primary act of mercy on the part of the blessed is to seek and yearn ad infinitum the mercy from the Redeemer Jesus. When Jesus becomes our Lord and Savior, there is no more condemnation. Indeed, Jesus removes our sins as far as the east is from the west. Yet without recognizing and repenting of our betrayals, we can never truly see the fulfillment that comes when grace is presented. We know well enough of our human frailty. However much we may stride to overcome temptations of the evil, many times we encounter tragic downfalls. Therefore there is a necessity for us to be always leaning on to Jesus's redemptive power and mercy. One preacher beautifully said, "While I am tossed over by the Evil, the only thing I do is just to hide behind the Cross." The author writes in his Imitation of Christ: "In what can I hope, then, or in whom ought I trust, save only in the great mercy of God and the hope of heavenly grace?"

In Jesus's life, we observe that all the sinners, who were bestowed the divine forgiveness, didn't stop with just confessing to Jesus; they continued to express their reciprocal love to him by different kinds of love deeds as penance and accepted willingly whatever the temporal punishment their sins yielded and God permitted. They obeyed as the Lord ordered them in love: "Go, sin no more." "Go and proclaim the praises of God." "Go and forgive your enemies." "Go and keep my commandment of love."

We should firmly believe that the costly grace of forgiveness is the sheer gratuitous gift of God. It is a gift of "amazing grace." We love to sing often: "Amazing grace how sweet the sound, that saved a wretch like me! I once was lost, but now am found, was blind, but now I see." Though God's love is unconditional, it breeds love. In other words, it surely affects the love line between God and the sinner. However, to appropriate it in daily life and to maintain it till we reach heaven, we have to stay on course of God's love. Since we are so vulnerable and even very unpredictable, we may be succumbed to evil forces. This is why a sinful man Saul, being converted to be Paul, recognized the necessity of Jesus's blood for forgiveness of sins and indicated his resolute will to live, not as old Saul, not even as new Paul, but as Christ living in him. Fully conscious of his human frailty, he preached to himself, saying,

> But if I am building up again those things
> that I tore down, then I show myself to be a
> transgressor. For through the law I died to

the law that I might live for God. I have been crucified with Christ; yet I live, no longer I, but Christ lives in me; insofar as I now live in the flesh, I live by faith in the Son of God who has loved me and given himself up for me. I do not nullify the grace of God; for if justification comes through the law, then Christ died for nothing. (Gal. 2:18–21)

Consequently the Apostle advised us to 'work out our salvation with fear and trembling'. (Phil. 2:12)

The Necessity of Importuning God's Mercy

Soliciting God's mercy every moment of our risky life is the best and most beneficial tactic for living a restful life. All the merciful deeds Jesus proposes to us in order to be blessed can possibly flow only out of this uninterrupted craving for the divine mercy. However much we may be pitying and sympathizing our neighbors, the acts of forgiving and tolerating their mistakes, blunders, and sins would be very difficult for us if we closely appended to the amazing grace. Jesus always observed the greatness of this grace. And that is why, while religious people like Simon the Pharisee were keen on finding fault with the public sinner, Jesus observed in her only the beauty of amazing grace (Luke 7:36–50): "Two different men looked at her, but saw totally different realities. One saw an immoral woman who deserved only to be rebuked and sent away. The other saw a grateful woman who had been liberated from the shame of an unfortunate life."

Persevere in Consciousness of God's Mercy

Acknowledging that we have committed sins against God, we should reach out to Him with a wholehearted, faith-filled, and love-oriented contrition: Humans, usually with their freedom and dignity, not easily acknowledge our sins and shortcomings. Good Lord knows it; therefore he tries his best to make us aware of it through his fellow servants. Remember this is what Jesus included in his parable about Lazarus and the rich man.

> When the rich man suffering torments in hell begged Abraham to send him to his father's house, so that he may warn five brothers who still live in the world with all their sins, lest they too come to this place of torment, Abraham replied, "They have Moses and the prophets. Let them listen to them." Again the rich man said, "Oh no, father Abraham, but if someone from the dead goes to them, they will repent." Then Abraham said, "If they will not listen to Moses and the prophets, neither will they be persuaded if someone should rise from the dead." (Luke 16:27–31)

The Bible contains so many incidents of God sending his messengers to the sinners to renew and reclaim the awareness of his grace. In the OT, we read that God used Nathan as his messenger to remind David how God felt hurt by his sin and we too see how David felt remorse of conscience. "David said to Nathan, 'I have sinned against the LORD'" (2 Sam. 12:7–13).

Secondly, even though God expects us to beg for his mercy often, about which we will be talking in next chapter, he longs for our recommitment to the basic covenantal treaty we spiritually made with him. The converted sinner David includes very often in most of his hymns of mercy like Psalm 51, an appeal for renewal of his heart or spirit: "A clean heart create for me, God; renew within me a steadfast spirit. Do not drive me from before your face, nor take from me your holy spirit. Restore to me the gladness of your salvation; uphold me with a willing spirit" (12–14). Human spirit is the seat of chesed; if this is properly kept secure, all external actions of humans would be never unholy and displeasing God.

The third suggestion I want to include, as the premier of all the tactics to preserve awareness of God's mercy, what Jesus dreamed of his disciples practicing their religion. He wanted anything we perform for appropriating the amazing grace must be done "in Spirit and in truth" (John 4:23). People wrongly interpret Jesus's words for their own advantage and according to their whims and fancies. In spirit is okay—as everyone considers, absolutely Jesus wants us to be sorry, to be contrite, to resolve, and to intercede within our spirit. However, he too adds the word *truth*. According to his religious values, we should interpret it validly that all that we do in religion must be truthful; this means we have to use both our spirit and our body. This is the total truth about humans. We are made of soul and body. God, though he is a Spiritual Being, demands from us while we still live in this earth to worship and relate to him by both elements we are made of. When one of them is missing, the other loses its strength and validity.

This is the reason Jesus was appreciating what the sinful woman did to him at the dinner table of Simon the Pharisee. She demonstrated her spirit of love to Jesus by her actions and gestures. Luke writes, "Bringing an alabaster flask of ointment, she stood behind him at his feet weeping and began to bathe his feet with her tears. Then she wiped them with her hair, kissed them, and anointed them with the ointment." Jesus praised her sacramental manner of expressing her love, contrition, and resolution.

When the others remarked about this lady's sacramental gesture toward the Lord, Jesus replied, "Do you see this woman? When I entered your house, you did not give me water for my feet, but she has bathed them with her tears and wiped them with her hair. You did not give me a kiss, but she has not ceased kissing my feet since the time I entered. You did not anoint my head with oil, but she anointed my feet with ointment." He too added, "I tell you, her many sins have been forgiven because she has shown great love."

CHAPTER 18

Our CHESED Action 2: Frequently Encountering God's Mercy

Contrite Spirit Is the Living Quarter of God's Mercy

"I am sorry" are three little words that have an almost incredible potential for transformation and yet these three little words seldom roll easily off the human tongue. Because of this, these three little words often go unsaid, and as a result, no transformation takes place. Instead, wounds fester, grudges grow, revenge is plotted, alienation grows. "I am sorry" is a difficult language to master, and fluency comes only to the humble, the simple, the truthful, and the strong. "I am sorry" is a challenge because these words admit of imperfection, and none of us wants to look very long into that "tell-all" mirror. "I am sorry" admits of weakness and failure; it says I am capable of wrongdoing, of hurting another person's feelings, sensibilities, reputation, and happiness. "I am sorry" admits that I am a work in progress. "I am sorry" chokes in the throat of those who dare to say it because these words say, "I am in need."

Often, our pride, guilt feeling, and fear prevent us from drawing close to the Lord and saying to him, "I am sorry." The English poet Alexander Pope once wrote, "To err is human, to forgive divine." That is why I often tell my congregations at somewhere at some time that both the amazing grace of God and the amazing stupidity of humans encounter each other at David's Camp of CHESED.

God, who is the high and lofty and holy one, has promised: "I dwell in a high and holy place, but also with the contrite and lowly of spirit, to revive the spirit of the lowly, to revive the heart of the crushed" (Isa. 57:15). We have to note here that the merciful God, who is supposed to pardon our sins and reconcile with us, promises that he will permanently dwell in our heart for reviving it. Another kind of divine anomaly in God's CHESED interactions with humans.

It is this heavenly promise, being read in the book of Isaiah, that sinners like King David, Paul, and public sinners like Magdalene, Matthew, and others like Augustine, heard in the recesses of their hearts. This is why they could return to the Lord again and again to receive God's merciful forgiveness. Jesus emphasized this regular way of getting forgiveness from his Father. He wanted it as a daily program of our earthly life like that of eating food. He included a petition of pleading for this grace to the Father in his Prayer: "Give us each day our daily bread and forgive us our sins" (Luke 11:3-4). As we pointed out earlier in this book, Jesus loved to be with this kind of sinners. When his righteous enemies complained against his dining with sinners, he plainly stated, "Those who are well do not need a physician, but the sick do. I did not come to call the righteous but sinners" (Mark 2:16-17).

149

He too pronounced many times his Father would be very much appreciative of tears falling down from the eyes of contrite sinners. In his parable on the Prayer of Mercy, comparing the arrogant attitude of the Pharisee and that of the tax collector, he is quoted as saying, "I tell you, the latter (who stood off at a distance and would not even raise his eyes to heaven but beat his breast and prayed, 'O God, be merciful to me a sinner') went home justified, not the former (Luke 18:13–14).

Daily Appropriating Forgiveness in Solitude

Every sin we commit is first and foremost personal. However much it would have occurred by bad influences, misbehaviors, and temptations of outsiders, our sin is our product, personally inherited from our own evil spirit. As result, we personally reap its repercussions and we also are bound personally to make rectification for restoration. The God who personally made covenant with me has to be approached personally for getting his reconciliation. This has to be done in solitude, with no distraction and distortion from outside.

In order to find mercy and forgiveness from God, we must humbly turn to him with all our burden of sins, confident that we will find acceptance and forgiveness. For this, Jesus's disciples must adhere to our Master's life and instructions in performing regular practices of mercy-filled heart-beating and as a result we will be counted among the blessed. In this effort of encountering God's merciful pardon, there are many role models in the Bible and in history.

We are trained through our catechism and Bible classes that when we become conscious of our sins, we need to do the act of contrition, which is one of the five penitential acts. In solitude, namely, being alone with God, either we recite a formal prayer of contrition like, "O my God, I am sorry for my sins because I have offended you. I know I should love you above all things. Help me to do penance, to do better, and to avoid anything that might lead me to sin. Amen."

We also can use a biblical prayer of contrition King David left with us (Ps. 51) in which he includes all that we need for encountering God's mercy. First, he begs God's mercy by saying, "Have mercy on me, God, in accord with your merciful love. (Have mercy upon me, O Elohim, according to Thy chesed (OJB). Then he deliberates his repugnance for the sins he has committed; he recognizes how he dirtied himself by them and requests the Lord to cleanse him and wash him thoroughly from all those stains. Finally we find him very sincere to his belief that God's mercy is unconditional and therefore he does not expose his resoluteness of not committing sins anymore; rather, he goes one step further, promising the Lord that he would try with God's help keep his heart good, holy and contrite. And that is the only kind of sin offering he will make to his God. We too can make use of any ejaculatory prayer such as "the Jesus Prayer," which has some biblical events of seeking Jesus's merciful support as its backdrop: "O Lord Jesus Christ, Son of the living God, have mercy on me, a sinner." This should be the nonstop heartbeats of the merciful; plus reading and meditating God's words of mercy-filled purification and restoration, which he has marvelously performed in history, especially through Jesus Christ.

I have heard many Christian preachers, especially the TV and online evangelists, highlight unequivocally that Christ purchased by his Blood our forgiveness and reconciliation and we can add nothing to give to Christ as condition to appropriate it except our faith. In addition, the same preachers never forget to add that it is fitting that we seize what he bought for us by prayer and confession every day.

Such regular confession of our sins and appealing God's grace of forgiveness expresses first that we are not faking as pharisaical righteous people; secondly, as John points out in his letter, we cannot be called liars before God. If we say "We have fellowship with him" while we continue to walk in darkness, we lie and do not act in truth. But if we walk in the light as he is in the light, then we have fellowship with one another and the blood of his Son Jesus cleanses us from all sin. If we say "We are without sin," we deceive ourselves, and the truth is not in us. If we acknowledge our sins, he is faithful and just and will forgive our sins and cleanse us from every wrongdoing. If we say "We have not sinned," we make him a liar, and his word is not in us (1 John 1:6–10). I am convinced when we confess our sins and our human weaknesses, simultaneously we too confess (acknowledge) the greatness of God's mercy and the holiness of his justice.

Frequently Getting God's Forgiving Mercy through the Church

Besides getting mercy from God in private, going to our inner room of the soul, closing the door of external noises, so that God in secret may repay us (ref. Matt. 6:6), we too must join the church community in pleading for the same. The valid reasons are as follows: We are social beings; we are elevated because of God's CHESED, to be affiliated to a chosen race, a royal priesthood, a holy nation, and a people of God's own (Ref. 1 Pet. 2:9). In this dignified membership, I, by my personal sins, taint the greatness of my community; every one of my sins, like an object dropped into a pond, effecting ripples across the water, can make malignant consequences through the entire community.

Another very important reason is that the church, established by Jesus, as a "field hospital." I see the church as a field hospital after battle. It is useless to ask a seriously injured person if he has high cholesterol and about the level of his blood sugars! You have to heal his wounds. Then we can talk about everything else. Heal the wounds, heal the wounds. . . . And you have to start from the ground up (Pope Francis). This wonderful and relevant papal metaphor for the church allows us to go deeper into the mystery of God's mercy found in the church.

We are blessed with being a member of the church, which is believed and trusted as the God-given resource for us for encountering Divine Mercy and become the blessed. This is a longstanding belief of Christianity; from its onset, Church is a structure, a realm, a place, a situation, and an instrument to receive forgiveness of sins from the mercy of God. Though in the Nicene Creed, formulated in the year 325 at the Council of Nicaea, we read, "We acknowledge one baptism for the forgiveness of sins," in Apostle's Creed, which, as the most common view is, was originally developed in the first or second century, we recite simply, "I believe in the forgiveness of sins."

Discussing about this magnificent role played by the church, *Catechism of the Catholic Church* proclaims:

> During his public life, Jesus not only forgave sins, but also made plain the effect of this forgiveness: he reintegrated forgiven sinners into the community of the People of God from which sin had alienated or even excluded them. A remarkable sign of this is the fact that Jesus receives sinners at his table, a gesture that expresses in an astonishing way both God's forgiveness and the return to the bosom of the People of God. (CCC 1443)

Plus, augmenting her claim that Jesus bestowed to her an unthinkable power to perform the mercy-giving task in the name of Divine Mercy, the church quotes Jesus's words to Peter to teach us: In imparting to his apostles his own power to forgive sins, the Lord also gives them the authority to reconcile sinners with the church. This ecclesial dimension of their task is expressed most notably in Christ's solemn words to Simon Peter: "I will give you the keys of the kingdom of heaven, and whatever you bind on earth shall be bound in heaven, and whatever you loose on earth shall be loosed in heaven."

> The office of binding and loosing which was given to Peter was also assigned to the college of the apostles united to its head. (CCC 1444)

> The words bind and loose mean: whomever you exclude from your communion, will be excluded from communion with God;

> whomever you receive anew into your
> communion, God will welcome back into his.
> Reconciliation with the Church is inseparable
> from reconciliation with God. (CCC, 1445)

In discussing and believing in the august role of the church, we never forget the eternal truth that Jesus the Savior of mankind is all-in-all taking all the roles in this hospital field, such as being its gate (John 10:7); acting as physician (Luke 5:31); handing out his Body and Blood as medication for healthy life (1 Cor. 11:28–30); undergoing bodily pains and sufferings as sources of healing sinful humanity (Isa. 53:4–5). Therefore, any human who gets sick out of sins can dare enough to enter into the church, Jesus's field hospital for both prevention and cure of human sinfulness. All the humans who are working in that hospital are only Jesus's representatives, performing all forgiving practices in *persona Christi* (in the person of Christ).

Forgetting the debate on how many such merciful forgiving practices (sacraments) Jesus offered to his church and on how those practices are performed on the basis of his good and eternal desire of establishing his Church as "field hospital" for all humans afflicted by sins, we can come out with four sacramental practices, which have been performed throughout church history, either formally or informally: baptism, Holy Communion, reconciliation, and anointing of the sick.

Encountering God's Mercy in Baptism

> Repent and be baptized, every one of you, in
> the name of Jesus Christ for the forgiveness of

your sins; and you will receive the gift of the
holy Spirit. (Acts 2:38)

That was how the Church was introduced as "field hospital" at its sunrise to both Israelites and the pagans. The sacrament of baptism, as all Christians believe, is not only a sort of christening or registering as a member of the church, but more than anything else is the common source of God's merciful forgiveness of all our sins. The Council of Florence called it "the gateway to life in the Spirit"; in Roman Catechism II, 2, 5 we read, "Baptism is the sacrament of regeneration through water in the word." Saint Gregory of Nazianzus, in his Oratio 40, 3-4, writes on the role of baptism:

> We call it gift, grace, anointing, enlightenment,
> garment of immortality, bath of rebirth, seal,
> and most precious gift. It is called gift because
> it is conferred on those who bring nothing of
> their own; grace since it is given even to the
> guilty; Baptism because sin is buried in the
> water; anointing for it is priestly and royal as
> are those who are anointed; enlightenment
> because it radiates light; clothing since it veils
> our shame; bath because it washes; and seal as
> it is our guard and the sign of God's Lordship.

In traditional baptism ceremony, there is a beautiful prayer that the minister recites, blessing the baptismal water reminding us how historically God used the waters as symbols of the baptism he would be offering us through his Son. Referring to Noah's Ark, by which only eight persons were saved, the prayer includes the following:

The waters of the great flood you made a
sign of the waters of Baptism, that make an
end of sin and a new beginning of goodness.
Also, indicating how OT Israel were liberated
through water, prayer adds: You freed the
children of Abraham from the slavery of
Pharaoh, bringing them dry-shod through the
waters of the Red Sea, to be an image of the
people set free in Baptism. (Ref. *Catechism of
the Catholic Church*)

Grace-Filled Meeting of God and Humans in the Eucharist

Holy Communion in the church has been one of
those regular sacraments through which we are told we
get healing of merciful forgiveness from the Lord. It is not
merely by lisping certain mercy-filled prayers during the
rite, but also through receiving the Eucharist. As many
medical doctors and Christian psychologists like Linda
Josef testify, through Holy Communion indeed people
have been healed of cancer, diabetes, Epstein-Barr virus,
and more (ref. her article in an online blog, Sid Roth's
IT'S SUPERNATURAL); however when we receive the
Body and Blood of Christ in worthy manner, we are
spiritually healed, namely, we feel that God by his mercy
has accepted us and reconciled with us.

Holy Communion, also called the Eucharist, was
originated in Jesus's Last Supper. That is what Paul
writes about handing on to his Christians the tradition
of sharing the Eucharist which he had received from the
Lord (1 Cor. 11:23–26). The Evangelist Matthew in his
Gospel spells out what Jesus's intention was in starting

this practice. According to him, Jesus breaking the bread and handing it out to his disciples said, "Take and eat; this is my body. While he gave them the cup of wine he added: . . . this is my blood of the covenant, which will be shed on behalf of many for the forgiveness of sins" (Matt. 21:26–28). Church tradition never hesitates to continue this rite in the spirit of Jesus adding a "prayer for spiritual healing" for the participants in the Holy Communion as a preparation: "Lord, I am not worthy that you should enter under my roof; but only say the word, and my soul shall be healed."

Fr. John Hampsch CMF, in his book on *The Healing Power of the Eucharist*, convinces us with his powerful, experiential tone that with our expectant faith, we can rely on the Eucharistic Lord for emotional, physical, and spiritual healing. He confirms that such healing power is present in the Eucharist by recounting so many testimonies to the miraculous healings done in many people's lives.

Saints like Alphonsus Liguori declare that "we must suffer and all must suffer be they just or be they sinners. Each one must carry his cross. He that carries the cross with patience is saved. The one who does not carry the cross with patience will not reach paradise." They are absolutely correct. Without undergoing our earthly sufferings, as Augustine remarked, we remain chaff for the burning hell and not wheat for the blissful heaven. As God demanded from his Son, so does he from us to endure the sufferings patiently. We know our limited capacity of such heroic endurance during sufferings. I agree with Fr. John A. Hardon, SJ, that without special grace from God, we cannot go through sufferings as to become true inheritors of God's mansions. Fr. Hardon writes in one of his articles in his blog on *Christ the Miracle Worker in the Eucharist*: The grace to practice even heroic patience comes from Jesus Christ in the Blessed Sacrament. Christ had to endure the agony of the cross to make the Holy Eucharist possible. It is especially from Him present on our altars in the Blessed Sacrament that we obtain a share in His power of enduring our crosses as the prelude of eternal glory.

Father Hardon, referring to various miracles that occurred in the early church, lists out some more miraculous gifts we receive from the Eucharist, such as the grace to be faithful on living a community life, living a life of selfless charity with other humans, and the moral power to live with people who are not amiable. Fr. Hardon, writing in the same article about the intellectual miracles happening through the Eucharist, inspires me with his succinct but experiential testimony on this matter. In his view, the human will is a blind faculty.

> We don't know with our wills alone what to choose, what to reject, what to love. Our wills must be enlightened by the mind and the mind must be enlightened by the mind of the Living God who became man. This will never happen wholistically by mere human endeavors. Only the Eucharist where the Son of Wisdom, Master of Teaching, and Super Man empowered with strong will but mendable by God's Will, presents. This is achieved by those people not only who are merely frequenting Holy Communion but mostly by those who have learned and tried to practice silent sitting in front of

the Blessed Sacrament which is the only place on earth that our minds are mainly enlightened by the mind of God is in the presence of God incarnate. This is how the Church have been blessed with great masters of Christian theology who obtained their superhuman grasp of the mysteries revealed by God from their meditation before Jesus Christ, Incarnate Truth present in the Blessed Sacrament.

CHESED *Restoration Deed in Confession*

Sacrament of Reconciliation is another source in the Church to encounter the merciful forgiveness of God in Jesus. Quoting from Vat. II Constitution *Lumen gentium*, *Catholic Catechism* introduces Church Traditional teaching on the Sacrament of Penance and Reconciliation, saying,

> Sin is before all else an offense against God, a rupture of communion with him. At the same time it damages communion with the Church. For this reason conversion entails both God's forgiveness and reconciliation with the Church, which are expressed and accomplished liturgically by the sacrament of Penance and Reconciliation. (1440)

Church tradition firmly holds that Jesus instituted the sacrament of penance through which sinful members of the Church, who have fallen into the cruel hands of the evil and consequently lost their baptismal grace and wounded ecclesial communion, graciously granted opportunities to convert and to recover from the evil force as often as they are in need. Tertullian, the church father, very well portrayed this fact in a metaphorical way: (this sacrament is) "the second plank after the shipwreck which is the loss of grace" (De Paenit. 4, 2: PL 1, 1343). That is why the church and her saints never cease to recommend regular attending of this sacrament, mainly because it is the truthful sacramental demonstration of humans' acknowledgement of sins, love-based contrition and willful resolve.

For a modern man and woman to go to confession is a great penance. But God longs to see us demonstrating our contrition and resolve in not only Spirit but also in body and this is how the action becomes total and holistic. Expounding this truthful truth more deeply, Augustine wrote,

> Whoever confesses his sins. . . is already working with God. God indicts your sins; if you also indict them, you are joined with God. Man and sinner are, so to speak, two realities: when you hear "man" - this is what God has made; when you hear "sinner" - this is what man himself has made. Destroy what you have made, so that God may save what he has made. . . . When you begin to abhor what you have made, it is then that your good works are beginning, since you are accusing yourself of your evil works. The beginning of good works is the confession of evil works. You do the truth and come to the light. (In Jo. ev. 12, 13)

When we go to confession, we express our appeal for God's mercy in faith and love. We see God and his Son demanded such gesture from sinful people. He likes the contrite heart; the broken heart filled with contrition. However, we need show this in truth, faith and love. The sacrament of reconciliation is one way to demonstrate this triple inner virtues wholly. Luke's Gospel story about Jesus, the Pharisee, and the Prostitute proves it.

There is the love of the sinful woman, who humbles herself before the Lord; her cry of repentance and joy washes the feet of the Master, and her hair dries them with gratitude; her kisses are pure expression of her affection; and the fragrant ointment poured out with abundance attests how precious He is to her eyes. This woman's every gesture speaks of love and expresses her desire to have an unshakeable certainty in her life: that of being forgiven. And Jesus gives this assurance: welcoming her, He demonstrates God's love for her, just for her! Love and forgiveness are simultaneous: God forgives her much, everything, because "she loved much" (Luke 7: 47); and she adores Jesus because she feels that in Him there is mercy and not condemnation. Thanks to Jesus, God casts her many sins away behind Him, He remembers them no more (cf. Is. 43:25). For her, a new season now begins; she is reborn in love, to a new life.

This woman has really met the Lord. In silence, she opened her heart to Him; in pain, she showed repentance for her sins; with her tears, she appealed to the goodness of God for forgiveness. For her, there will be no judgment except that which comes from God, and this is the judgment of mercy. The protagonist of this meeting is certainly the love that goes beyond justice. Simon the Pharisee, on the contrary, cannot find the path of love.

He stands firm upon the threshold of formality. He is not capable of taking the next step to go meet Jesus, who brings him salvation. Simon limited himself to inviting Jesus to dinner, but did not really welcome Him. In his thoughts, he invokes only justice, and in so doing, he errs. His judgment on the woman distances him from the truth and does not allow him even to understand who guest is. He stopped at the surface; he was not able to look to the heart.

However, Simon was shown as a good-hearted man. After Jesus narrated a tiny parable, his question of which a servant would love his master most, the Pharisee answered correctly, "The one, I suppose, whose larger debt was forgiven." And Jesus didn't fail to acknowledge the Pharisee's right judgment: "You have judged rightly" (Luke 7:43). Unfortunately Simon's judging attitude had not enhanced by love and mercy. The basic quest of a religious person is to be righteous or to be justified, namely, to be in the right with God. While so many of humans try to get themselves right with God by keeping certain laws and rituals, we, Christians, believe with Paul that we are justified not by the works of the law but through faith in Jesus Christ. It means that this justification is something not to be earned but to be received as a gift. Justification by the grace-full act of God in Christ is apprehended by humans through faith alone. Jesus says to a sinner who repents: "Your faith has saved you; go in peace" (Luke 7: 50).

Through this "forgiving event," Jesus pointed out to us who are searching for his merciful forgiveness that God's unconditional mercy expects our CHESED-response in the spirit of faith, and love, and in truth.

In Human Weakness God's **CHESED** *Sparkles by Anointing*

As the fourth resource in the Church for coming into contact with God's mercy and his forgiveness is the sacrament of the anointing of the sick. The most opportune and needy time for experiencing God's mercy is none other than the hours of human suffering, sickness, and dying. In those hours, we observe more intensively our powerlessness, our limitations, and our fragility and finitude. I have experienced and so with all my brothers and sisters whom I was serving as their spiritual counselor for four decades how we are led by those critical situations to anguish and pain not only physically, but more mentally and spiritually, which many times take us to despair and aversion for the Creator. Indeed for most of us, who are strenuously serving God, trusting in his immeasurable goodness, those times make us more mature; we feel those occasions offer us chances to retrospect our deeper selves and start discerning what is most essential in our lives, namely, we feel a longing for more intensively and sincerely related to the Almighty.

During that process of self-analysis, most of us discover we have deviated and drifted far away from God's Way. Our hearts ache at those times to return and reconcile with God. God in Jesus, the most bountiful in mercy, warmly waiting for our returns. This is the backdrop of the age-old Church practice of anointing of the sick. It all began when our Lord was traveling in Palestine with his disciples. The Bible highlights that God is the Master of life and death, but never intends his people to die eternally though they die physically.

Jesus desired his followers should never lose hope when they get sickness, even leading to death. That was his Gospel brought from his Father. He preached about it and in season and out of season went around demonstrated this hope-filled Gospel through his healing deeds. Among many such healings there are some like the event Mark narrates in his Gospel (2:5–11) pinpoint the intrinsic link existing physical healing to spiritual cleansing and forgiving. Encouraging the paralytic man, sickened by sins as the public judged, Jesus proposed to him first and foremost: "Child, your sins are forgiven." He too affirmed he had twofold authority within him to bestow physical cure as well as merciful forgiveness of sins for all humans. In various occasions he too compared human sinfulness is literally a sickness that can be cured by him as a heavenly Physician (Mark 2:17).

We don't think Jesus did his ministries of healing and forgiving by "anointing with oil," but we know he did most of them by some signs to heal. As Gospels tell us, he used "laying on of hands," spittle, mud, and washing, and so on. But when he sent his seventy-two disciples ahead of him in pairs to every town and place he intended to visit, he delegated the power to perform this mercy-filled healing rite to the sick and driving out of demons. Mark writes that these disciples "drove out many demons, and they anointed with oil many who were sick and cured them." According to Bible scholars, "anointing with oil" was a common medicinal remedy in Jesus's time but seen here as a vehicle of divine power for healing.

This conviction took strong root in the life of the Church, and as James testifies in his letter, it has become a permanent sacramental ritual for the sick and the dying for the forgiveness of sins.

> Is anyone among you sick? He should summon the presbyters of the church, and they should pray over him and anoint [him] with oil in the name of the Lord, and the prayer of faith will save the sick person, and the Lord will raise him up. If he has committed any sins, he will be forgiven. (Jas. 5:14–15)

The words and gestures used in conferring this sacrament of anointing of the sick portrays its reality and beneficial effects on the sick people. The minister anointing the sick on their forehead and hands with duly blessed oil says, "Through this holy anointing may the Lord in his love and mercy help you with the grace of the Holy Spirit. May the Lord who frees you from sin save you and raise you up" (CIC, Can. 847 § 1).

CHAPTER 19

＊＊❀❀▦▶━━━━━━━━❀━━━━━━━━◀▦❀❀＊＊

CHESED Action 3:
Unreservedly Forgiving Those
Who Hurt Us

In the first two chapters of this section, we have been discussing how to solicit and encounter God's mercy in order to be blessed. Later in this section, we would be treating on the merciful acts, spiritual and corporal, through which we would add golden feather to the crown of our blessedness. In between those chapters, we need to hash out the core of the requirements to achieve this highest honor. Let us now go straight to Jesus's clarion call for all his followers about how to conduct ourselves being 'merciful' in order to become 'the blessed' both in this world and the world to come. We know well enough the great promises of Jesus for us through which he underlined that the merciful as we are we will get into his heavenly mansions after this earthly life; he wished the merciful also the same blessed life of joy and peace in this world. As Paul Boese wrote, "Forgiveness does not change the past, but it does enlarge the future."

Soon after, Jesus ordered us to be merciful just as our Father is merciful; he explained how to be merciful as God, saying, "Stop judging and you will not be judged. Stop condemning and you will not be condemned. Forgive and you will be forgiven" (Luke 6:37). We should note here that Jesus's main advice to us is the positive act of forgiving others, which means to stop judging and condemning them.

The Act of Forgiving Is the Primary Mercy Effect

Among the various mercy effects of God's CHESED in human life, one that is consistently testified in the Bible and church tradition is the amazing grace through which God forgives all our sins; as a Father to his children, he overlooks all our imperfections and defects and not only does he forget our past misdeeds, but he also asks us to forget them but expects us always to remain in his love and trust. In my seminary days, I used to go to my spiritual father and trying my best to enlist my past confessed sins that were annoying me.

After many times exhorting me patiently that I needed not to do this because God has forgiven all of them already, one day he stood up and seriously looked at me and offered me a wise advice. He said, "Whatever is in your past, whatever you have done and the devil keeps throwing it up in your face; however you need to know that God was standing at the window and he saw the whole thing; he has seen your whole life. He wants you to know that he loves you and that you are forgiven. Ben, the only thing God is worried about you is just wondering how long you will let the devil make a slave of you." That was the day I was liberated from not only my scrupulosity but also my pride and ignorance.

Jesus too insisted we have to remain in his love after we encounter God's mercy. Loving his Father and himself cannot be imagined by him without loving our neighbors. This is why as the only new commandment he handed down to us, he exhorted us to love our neighbors as he loved us. The highest point of neighborly love according to him is forgiving our neighbors.

Forgiving neighborly enemies or inimical neighbors, he said in the Sermon on the Mount: "Blessed are the merciful; for they will be shown mercy" (Matt. 5:7). He included in that Sermon his special prayer to the Father in which he wanted us to pray . . . forgive us our debts, as we forgive our debtors (Matt. 6:12). In order to emphasize the importance of this petition, he expounded it: "If you forgive others their transgressions, your heavenly Father will forgive you. But if you do not forgive others, neither will your Father forgive your transgressions" (Matt. 6:14–15). Matthew also includes Jesus's saying about forgiveness that corrected, enhanced, and elevated the Jewish former way of thinking about the command of loving neighbors:

> You have heard that it was said, "You shall love your neighbor and hate your enemy." But I say to you, love your enemies, and pray for those who persecute you, that you may be children of your heavenly Father, for he makes his sun rise on the bad and the good, and causes rain to fall on the just and the unjust. (Matt. 5:43–45)

To make this hardest demand from heaven to be grasped even the little ones, he made use of a parable about the "unforgiving servant" and at the end he stated as its moral: "Should you not have had pity on your fellow servant, as I had pity on you? Then in anger his master handed him over to the torturers until he should pay back the whole debt. So will my heavenly Father do to you, unless each of you forgives his brother from his heart (Matt. 18:21–35).

Before he narrated the parable, Peter being confused with such staggering requirement of forgiving others in order to become "the blessed," asked him, "If my brother sins against me, how often must I forgive him? And he replied, I say to you, not seven times but seventy-seven times" (Matt. 18:21–12). In other words, he wanted us to forgive countless times.

All the above-listed words of Jesus included in Matthew's Gospel. There is a valid reason to it. Matthew, as we know from the Bible, was a public sinner, not only being converted but also being elected as an apostle by the abundant mercy of Jesus. Humans as we are, we should know what would have happened in Matthew's life after his conversion and elevation. As the righteous people like Pharisees made a big uproar on this merciful action of Jesus, surely even among Jesus's followers some would have rejected Matthew as a sort of unclean person; besides, Matthew would have been struggling all the time to forgive those who rejected him and hated him. Naturally, these personal experiences would have moved him to collect many anecdotes and sayings of Jesus on showing mercy to others.

In addition to Matthew's collection of events and sayings on Jesus's" "forgiving mercy," Luke on his part went far ahead and got sight of what Jesus had taught on the showing mercy to others. In the Sermon on the Plain, his own version of the Sermon on the Mount, Luke includes Jesus's teaching on the "love of our enemies," and at the end he quotes Jesus's very demanding ideal of showing mercy for our coveting "the blessedness": "Be merciful, just as [also] your Father is merciful" (Luke 6:36). Since Luke was aware of the struggle we would be facing in living an unfeasible ideal of being merciful as our God, he added an unthinkable exemplary gesture of our Master becoming number one realizer of this superambitious act of forgiving even his enemies at the peak of his ignominious passion. He quotes Jesus as saying on the Cross: "Father, forgive them, they know not what they do" (Luke 23:34). Because of his final but most unthinkable public act of forgiving his enemies, the entire humanity of various faiths have been honoring Jesus over the centuries as the greatest person of mercy ever lived. Great people like Mahatma Gandhi, an orthodox Hindu, has confirmed his admiration for "forgiving" Jesus and he has alluded such heroic venture as an inspiration to uphold the strategy of 'non-violence' in his efforts to liberate India from British Rule. And up to this day, we can list out thousands of such nonviolent champions, who, despite being tortured, humiliated, thrown into prison, and even bleeding to death, have been forgiving their enemies with a smile such as Martin Luther King Jr. and Nelson Mandela and so on.

Unquestionably, millions of Jesus disciples in Church history fascinated by their Master's "kind of incredible action of forgiveness," like Deacon Stephan who, as he was stoned to death by his enemies, fell on his knees and cried out in a loud voice, "Lord, do not hold this sin against them" (Acts 7:60). I am sure more than anything, Stephan had performed as deacon of charities; this final act would have very much delighted God and his Master Jesus. The same chivalrous action has been the unique hallmark of Christianity. Very sadly, many Christians do not witness to it. It is because of inaptitude, ignorance, or hyperemotionality. Since they don't care for this magnificent deed, they miss both the true forgiveness from God and the blessedness promised by Jesus. Besides, what Jesus demands from his disciples regarding the act of forgiving is very hard to observe, namely, stop judging and stop condemning.

Human Reasons for Judging Others

First of all, there is an innate tendency in us to pronounce judgments on our neighbors. In biblical truth, we are made with the potentials to discern good and bad happening in and around us; unfortunately, we are hastier doing this against our fellowmen than against ourselves. Our minds, made of strong "Mosaic" blocks, hurry to sit on the judgment seat while we notice any evils done by others. Worse it would be when those evils are targeted at us and hurting us. Another reason for our judging others is that socially we cannot but live together as family, community or nation. Those around whom we live and move are different from each other, except being human like us, they individually look strange, speak strange, and act strange; therefore we feel or we are told by our elders that we should always watch out others around us closely and try to protect ourselves secure and safe. This is nothing but a norm of human survival. Unfortunately, since every human is a mystery by himself or herself, it is very hard to pass right and proper judgment on their behavior. Inevitably we cannot fully read their mind, and we cannot accurately know their motivation and thought behind their doings. But still as our survival demands some hold on our safety consideration over others, we hasten to judge them but most of the time we make wrong judgments.

The third reason for frequently judging others comes from the basic human need of self-esteem. Every human is born with dignity and therefore there exists in every one a demand to be respected and even to be exalted. Due to some twisted formation and by bitter or sweet experiences in life some of us would be too much craving for being esteemed by everybody we meet. Those crazy people are called spoiled brats. There are also others among us who by the same sources but in more or worse degree have developed a low-esteem profile about themselves. In common both groups of people are imbalanced twitters who struggle to make out an equilibrium of life. Either feeling jealous of others or being hateful of themselves they, misusing their ability to judge, begin to feel the others as competitors, opponents, and enemies. Such an inimical attitude energizes them to spoil the good name of others by spreading bad news and juicy gossips or even sometimes try to destroy others' families, and the communities they belong to.

The Fateful Flaw in Our Judging

The term *enemy* is defined in our dictionaries as one "unfriendly opponent who hates or seeks to harm somebody or something or even something that is harmful or obstructive." Enemies are not born; rather they are made by human beings' ignorance, limitation, selfishness, weakness, and so on. For convenience, let us call them the "converted enemies." They are the ones whom we judge as sinful, alien, unworthy to live and hold our hands. In other words, beyond ourselves there is no enemy at all. We, with our selfish shortsightedness, name our neighbors as enemies. But in themselves they are not. As any other humans the so-called enemies also have their needs. Especially they are in need of a merciful and compassionate touch from God through us. Indeed they are truly our neighbors. One of the modern spiritual writers says about God's heart: "In the beginning God said to Cain: What have you done to your brother Abel? On the last day He will not turn to Cain but to Abel saying 'What have you done to your brother Cain?'" Abel will not rise for revenge, but to guard Cain. The new earth will be when the victims will take care of their executioners. This is the heart of God. Jesus suggests to us to come out of our self-centered shortsightedness and to love the wrongly-named enemies as our neighbors.

Enmity or hatred is created in day today dealings among ourselves. Most of the time humans make our own neighbors as our enemies. In the parable Good Samaritan, for example, Jesus points out two enemies, the priest and the Levite, who did not help their neighbor who was in need, because they already have been prejudiced against their neighbor as an outcast and untouchable and even as public sinner. Surprisingly those two "righteous" neighbors behaved toward the needy person in such a hatred way that they made themselves as enemies to the neighbor. It is nothing but a ripple effect of hatred.

Secondly in order to encounter those 'converted enemies' in our petty world we play hurtful, tactful sometimes destructive games against them. Some of us forgive our enemies but never forget their names. Many also despise our enemies strategically, but respect them tactically. There are others who, after confronting our enemies at their den very smilingly, leave the room with a heavy step but spent the whole night and morning designing graves for them.

These "converted enemies" are not existing outside of us; rather they are at our door, in our family, in our community and in the nation. When our neighbors start behaving strange, appear strange, very truly reaching out to us in their needs, with our puny judgmental attitude we make enemies.

Divine Reasons for Not Judging Others

This is why God admonishes us to be careful in human acts of judging. In contrast to how humans misinterpret and abuse the power of judging, the revealed words of God accentuate some divine reasons why we should not judge others. Primarily, they urge us while we the sinners gravely need and seek forgiveness from the Holy and Almighty God we should never forget his Sovereignty. He has his own "territory" and therefore we should first give respect to it. God is the universal King, creating and directing and running the whole show of the creations.

That is what Jewish pilgrims were singing with David in gusto: "Declare among the nations: The Lord is king. The world will surely stand fast, never to be shaken. He rules the peoples with fairness" (Ps. 96:10). Our Creator, the immensely merciful God, as we deliberated in the second section of this book, is also just and faithful. In OT, all sacred writers, the Kings, the Prophets and the Judges, spell out the Creator's absolute authority to pass judgment over his creatures as Moses wrote God, telling him: "Vengeance is mine and recompense, for the time they lose their footing" (Deut. 32:35). Isaiah professed his faith in God's exclusive power to judge us very candidly: "For the Lord is our judge; the Lord is our lawgiver, the Lord is our king; he it is who will save us" (Isa. 33:22). The wise Teacher Sirach in his book categorically states the sole right of God either to recompense, or to requite and to punish humans: "The vengeful will face the Lord's vengeance; indeed he remembers their sins in detail" (Sir. 28:1).

Following those inspirational words of sacred writers, goodwilled people never ceased to confess with hope the final judgment God would pronounce against all malicious people: Sing before the Lord who comes, who comes to govern the earth, to govern the world with justice and the peoples with faithfulness (Ps. 96:13). Jesus, the begotten Son of God, being in agreement to all the OT revelations on God's singular supremacy in judging any humans, augmented it in his response to the one who came to him for settling some brotherly but greedy dispute saying: "Friend, who appointed me as your judge and arbitrator?" (Luke 12:13-14). He also disclaimed himself being compared to his Father in any way: As he was setting out on a journey, a man ran up, knelt down before him, and asked him, "Good teacher, what must I do to inherit eternal life?" Jesus answered him, "Why do you call me good? No one is good but God alone" (Mark 10:17-18).

Concurrently, Jesus, the Word becoming Flesh, never hesitated to acknowledge his partnership in the works of judging the humans, teaming with his Father. Nor does the Father judge anyone, but he has given all judgment to his Son, so that all may honor the Son just as they honor the Father (John 5:22-23). He always showed his humility and dependence to his Almighty Father by connecting his every action of judging to God's will.

> I cannot do anything on my own; I judge as
> I hear, and my judgment is just, because I do
> not seek my own will but the will of the one
> who sent me. (John 5:30)

He was categorical in his conviction that all that he does in judging humans are sound and indisputable. And even if I should judge, my judgment is valid; the reasons he listed out were two:

> One, because I am not alone, but it is I and
> the Father who sent me; two, you judge by
> appearances, but I do not judge anyone. (John
> 8:15-16)

In the light of above-cited biblical words, we can never argue against the eternal truth that the sovereign authority of judging humans belongs only to God and his Son and we the humans have no right over it. Every human is the child and the servant of God and the sibling of Jesus; therefore as Paul insists, no human on earth can pass judgment over the other. Who are you to pass judgment on someone else's servant? Before his own master he stands or falls. And he will be upheld, for the Lord is able to make him stand (Rom. 14:4). Apostle James repeats this fact more emphatically: "There is only one lawgiver and judge, he who is able to save and to destroy. But who are you to judge your neighbor?" (James 4:12).

Merciful Forgiving Instead of Judging

More than any other humans, the disciples of Jesus are conscious of the evils generated by agents of Satan and are victimized and persecuted by the evil-agents' violence, cruelty, puffed-up self. All Apostles and committed followers of Jesus demonstrated in their lives by their words and deeds the precious 'blessedness' inherited only by mercy-filled forgiving our enemies.

First they advised us that when somebody inflicts pain and sufferings to us, the only thing we can do is to hand him/her over to the hands of the Supreme Judge. I charge you in the presence of God and of Christ Jesus, who will judge the living and the dead, and by his appearing and his kingly power (2 Tim. 4:1). This is because we totally agree with Apostle James's contention: There is one lawgiver and judge who is able to save or to destroy. Who then are you to judge your neighbor? (James 4: 12).

Secondly, Love and truth will meet; justice and peace will kiss. Truth will spring from the earth; justice will look down from heaven. This NABRE version of Psalm 85:11–12 is translated in some other online Divine Office blog catholicexchange.com as: Kindness and faithfulness have met together, justice and peace have kissed. Faithfulness has sprung from the earth, and justice has looked down from heaven. I like the latter version which is very close to the core of our discussion on CHESED' in this book. The terms *kindness* (love, mercy) and *faithfulness* (truth), *justice* (righteousness) and *peace* are, according to biblical revelation, the constituents of the idealistic vision of the Kingdom of God. Therefore, as dedicated members of the Kingdom of God Jesus inaugurated, we can never leave out the spirit of mercy in every bit of our action toward our neighbors. If we want to be righteous, perfect, and holy like our Father and our Brother Jesus, we need to be mercy-filled just and justice-blended merciful.

As I pointed out previously in this chapter, we become culprits of making worse and false judgments against others wrongly imagining we do the 'just' thing. We know even God doesn't relate himself with us only on the basis of justice. How much more we his creatures should handle the gift of judging rightly and sensibly. Wisdom of God admonishes us through Sirach in this matter:

> Forgive your neighbor the wrong done to you;
> then when you pray, your own sins will be
> forgiven. Does anyone nourish anger against
> another and expect healing from the LORD?
> Can one refuse mercy to a sinner like oneself,
> yet seek pardon for one's own sins? If a mere
> mortal cherishes wrath, who will forgive his
> sins? (Sir. 28:2-5)

Nonetheless, when we judge others mercifully, we overcome our own attitudes of pride, jealousy, and violence and especially we win our enemies and offer them a chance to join God's Kingdom. It is good to quote Paul here who splendidly describe the positive effects of our merciful forgiveness of others:

> Do not repay anyone evil for evil; be concerned for what is noble in the sight of all. If possible, on your part, live at peace with all. Beloved, do not look for revenge but leave room for the wrath . . . Do not be conquered by evil but conquer evil with good. (Rom. 12:17–21)

He also included in his Letter a very tough advice quoting from OT: "If your enemies are hungry, give them food to eat, if thirsty, give something to drink; for live coals you will heap on their heads, and the LORD will vindicate you" (Prov. 25:21–22). This is what I mean whenever we forgive our inimical neighbors and show them some positive gesture of love, they in turn become rejuvenated in spirit by God's grace that is infused to them through us! We should never forget the saying of Saint Faustina: Let our judgment of souls cease, for God's mercy upon them is extraordinary.

Ultimately, the gracious act of forgiving our neighbors, whatever be their sinful condition is or however much we have been hurt by their misdeeds, must be practiced by the deep understanding and evergreen remembrance of our last days; of our death and decay; of the Lord's commandments (Sir. 28:6).

All the above-said reasons are for any human being who adheres to God through different religions. There is a most compelling reason for Jesus's disciples who believe and follow the exalted Jesus as their Lord and God to forgive others. Namely, we, the disciples of Jesus, are intrinsically connected to the covenant of the Most High (Sir. 28:7), namely, to his CHESED with us through his Son Jesus. Our forgiveness of others comes out of our intimate connections with God the Most High. First of all, both God and ourselves have made covenant with each other in Jesus and therefore we have to live up to that promise. As Sirach points out, we have to remember the Most High's covenant and overlook faults. In addition, we Christians are baptized in Christ Jesus. Therefore we live, move and have our being through him, with him and in him. All that we do and say should occur in that environment. As Paul writes, "If we live or die we live or die only in Christ. We do not live or die for ourselves." In other words, such deeper love and union with Christ makes us lose our very self, including its prestige, respect and glory. Most of the time we are hurt terribly by others only because they hurt our self-prestige, good name or good life. But as Christians our entire life and death belongs to Christ. Our glory, our prestige and our good name come only by our union with Christ and not at all from our neighbors, good and bad. So others' sins or evil deeds against us do not in any way affect us.

Being merciful to others and becoming the blessed demands from us certain obligations in our judging deals with our neighbors:

Mercifully Forgiving and Not Judicially Condemning

If we listen to Jesus carefully when he exhorts us in the matter of judging others, he never intends that we should avoid judging others at all cost. Rather he wants us to judge others as he judges them in truth and kindness.

While he candidly stated that he judged correctly the nature of humans. While many began to believe in his name when they saw the signs he was doing, as John writes, Jesus would not trust himself to them because he knew them all, and did not need anyone to testify about human nature. He himself understood it well (John 2:23-25). He too never avoided to deliberate the dignity and greatness of humans. Even the hairs of your head are all numbered. Fear not; you are of more value than many sparrows (Luke 12:7). Since he was fully aware of both the strength and weakness of humans he persuaded every human being to esteem, love and judge equally. He reiterated the one and only great love-command of the Father: Love God wholeheartedly and love fellowmen as yourself (Mark 12:31). In addition, we know Jesus explained how we should obey the command of equal love. For this, he said that we must keep him as our role model. I give you a new commandment: love one another. As I have loved you, so you also should love one another (John 13:34).

Elaborating Jesus's advice on how to judge others rightly, Apostles wrote their comments in their Letters. Paul confirms what the Lord's esteem about human glorious status: For we are his workmanship, created in Christ Jesus for good works, which God prepared beforehand, that we should walk in them (Eph. 2:10). However, he writes that we should have right approach in judging ourselves and others as well: Do nothing out of selfishness or out of vainglory; rather, humbly regard others as more important than yourselves. (Phil. 2: 3) For by the grace given to me I tell everyone among you not to think of himself more highly than one ought to think, but to think soberly, each according to the measure of faith that God has apportioned (Rom. 12:3). Paul too hands out a "rule of new life" to Jesus's disciples who, having stripped of their old self, put on a renewed life: Be angry but do not sin; do not let the sun set on your anger, and do not leave room for the devil (Eph. 4:26–27).

Never Judging Others at the First Sight

From the exhortation of Jesus as expounded by Paul, we know God to uphold a new kind of approach in judging others. We should never judge others with the feudalistic attitude of "killing at sight." We hear the Lord telling the Prophet Samuel while he was trying to recruit a worthy candidate for the first kingly seat: Do not look on his appearance or on the height of his stature, because I have rejected him. For the Lord sees not as man sees: man looks on the outward appearance, but the Lord looks on the heart (1 Sam. 16:7). I never cease to preach about this fact of Christian approach. As humans, being endowed with wisdom and capacity to judge, we are prone to pass judgment over others at the first sight of their misdeeds. But in the light of Christ we too have inherited by Baptism a new sight, capable of judging differently and positively and rightly. Hence if we are truly committed disciples of Jesus we stop judging at our natural first sight; pass for a few seconds; open the second brighter sight; and follow that light in our judging.

This second sight would remind us immediately who we are; and who others are in front of the Almighty. This is why Jesus preached on the Mountain: Judge not, that you be not judged. For with the judgment you pronounce you will be judged, and with the measure you use it will be measured to you (Matt. 7:-2). If we are normal persons who possess a well-balanced self-esteem we would accept with humility and honesty that we are born sinful and grown sinners. We know our limitations; we fail in many temptations; we fall and dirty ourselves and become unholy and unworthy to enter into the holy God's relationship. Why do you see the speck that is in your brother's eye, but do not notice the log that is in your own eye? Or how can you say to your brother, 'Let me take the speck out of your eye,' when there is the log in your own eye? You hypocrite, first take the log out of your own eye, and then you will see clearly to take the speck out of your brother's eye" (Matt. 7:3-5).

Tolerating Others' Difference but Accepting Their Goodness

I heard a story from one of the mission preachers who came to my parish. In a religion class of 5th grade students, teacher emphatically stated to the kids "only Catholics go to Heaven." While the whole class was silent, a boy got up and in no uncertain terms declared, "I know my mother is going to Heaven." "Well of course she is," teacher said. The boy retorted, "Well, my mother is not Catholic." His teacher, showing her face, frowned and looking completely confused asked him, "How can she not be Catholic, she is so good?" The teacher knew the woman who has been quietly and with no remuneration doing all the mending and altering of the church, convent and presbytery clothes and habits! Tolerance of strangers and acceptance of their goodness, as we discussed earlier, is not human nature. It takes downpour of divine grace showered from the mercy of God. Any grace of that kind cannot fall upon us until our ears and hearts listen to the words of God. Word of God is the two-edged sword that can break open any stubborn, hardheaded attitudes of humans.

The Word incarnate has spelt out about his relationship among us. He can relate to us as his father, mother, brother, sister and friend. But he put a condition to it. He will establish his such lovely and lively relationship only with those who hear the word of God and act on it (Luke 8:19–21). That is Jesus's micro and macrofamily system. In this system of Jesus there are too many strangers, so many barbarians, countless pagans, and numerous public sinners and criminals. Are we not stupid and blushed many times when we observe in day today life and read in histories that millions, outside our campuses of race, creed and clubs, are the "doers of Creator's Will" working night and day to enhance this world, this universe and trying to make this world a better place for their future generations? Thinking of the highest value of Jesus's family system we must prudently ignore the difference existing between us and so-called strangers, and ready to hug them, tolerate them and even accept them into our friendly company, if not our micro-family.

Giving Always Second Chances for Others' Renewal

Many times we feel like Peter frustrated over the blunders and hurts repeated by others. Peter approaching Jesus asked him, Lord, if my brother sins against me, how often must I forgive him? As many as seven times? Jesus bestowed us some burdensome but fruitful advice. I say to you, not seven times but seventy-seven times (Matt. 18:21–22). After his baffling answer Jesus explained himself with a parable on the unforgiving servant who was punished with cruel torturing for his merciless behavior. At the end of the story Jesus included the why of such repeated acts of forgiving. His only preoccupation was that we, his disciples, should win the ultimate 'blessedness' and not punishment. He said: So will my heavenly Father do to you, unless each of you forgives his brother from his heart (Matt. 18:23–35).

There are many in our society who won't accept the possibility that people can change? They are not willing to give people a second chance. A culture that doesn't believe in redemption is a culture without hope. With compassion and forgiveness we have to relate ourselves to the persons whom we consider as sinners. To reclaim a person is a delicate and difficult task. We have to learn to see the goodness in one another, and affirm that. People's faults can be cured only by loving them. We cannot change anyone unless we accept them as they are. Condemnation does not liberate; it oppresses. Jesus therefore desired we should connect ourselves to our neighbors in merciful spirit and tolerating their blunders embrace them with love. This does not mean we should endorse the evils they have produced; rather behave as our Father who loves sinners but hates the sin.

Offering Mercy-Oriented Correction

God is not all a goody-goody Papa, ignoring and leaving the humans in their sinful condition. Instead of the eternal whip of punishment, he has been always made recourse to slow, gradual but steady efforts to correct them. From the beginning of the world he had been doing this through his Prophets and his agents but later, when his Son came to this world, he entrusted the same divine procedure of converting sinners through mercy of the Church and her members. After preaching about God's immense merciful shepherding act of being in search of his strayed sheep, and stating categorically that it is not the will of your heavenly Father that one of these little ones be lost (Matt. 18:10–14), Jesus offers his followers the gentle and gradual way of dealing in correcting our sinful neighbors:

> If your brother sins against you, go and tell him his fault, between you and him alone. If he listens to you, you have gained your brother. But if he does not listen, take one or two others along with you, that every charge may be established by the evidence of two or three witnesses. If he refuses to listen to them, tell it to the church. And if he refuses to listen even to the church, let him be to you as a Gentile and a tax collector. (Matt. 18:15–17)

It is a pity many of us are stuck to our old attitudes or accomplishments or undertakings as our comfortable zone to travel peacefully in life. But we don't understand how much damage we do to our own and as well as others' spiritual walkathon. Spiritually we become dead while we socially and ritually thrive. As a consequence whatever we produce in the name of even God and religion-our words, decisions and actions, turned out to be poisonous and create a bigger chasm between the Living God and his people. Such unconscious agents of evil are belligerent to the Lord's marvelous deeds of progress and development among his humans. The saddest matter is this kind of people are found among many leaders in humanity, worst in religious circles. In a talk to the synod gathering recently Pope Francis referred to this tragedy even in the Church. He said these sort of people, with "closed hearts which frequently hide even behind the Church's teachings or good intentions, in order to sit in the chair of Moses and judge, sometimes with superiority and superficiality, difficult cases" of people of God.

One section of these intolerable people call themselves as fundamentalists about whom the journalists questioned Pope's opinion, he remarked, "Fundamentalism is an illness found in all religions. We have some in the Church, No, not some—a lot who believe they have the absolute truth and go around sullying others through calumny, defamation." The call of Jesus pushes each of us never to stop at the surface of things, especially when we are dealing with a person. We are called to look beyond, to focus on the heart to see how much generosity everyone is capable. No one can be excluded from the mercy of God; everyone knows the way to access it and the Church is the house that welcomes all and refuses no one. Its doors remain wide open, so that those who are touched by grace can find the certainty of forgiveness. The greater the sin, so much the greater must be the love that the Church expresses toward those who convert.

Forgetting the Hurts but Praying for Those Hurting

Regarding this issue of forgiving and forgetting others' sins I read a relevant advice from an unknown source:

Write your injuries in the sand, kindness in marble. Jesus has repeatedly demonstrated his wish for his followers not only by his deeds but also by saying that they should forgive their enemies and that as the Father and he has been doing love them and pray for them (Matt. 5:44).

We read in OT about the law of talion, "If injury ensues, you shall give life for life, eye for eye, tooth for tooth, hand for hand, foot for foot, burn for burn, wound for wound, stripe for stripe" (Exod. 21:23–25). Indeed, we should note the law of talion was not held up as a general principle to be applied throughout the book of the covenant nor it has been applied literally in Israel. However as some group of the Jews in his time were abusing this law in order to show off their righteousness and justice, Jesus challenged us to find a deeper form of justice than the supposed equilibrium offered by talion. He insisted there should be no resistance to the one who is evil; instead of hating the "converted enemies" he ordered us to love our enemies, and pray for those who persecute us (Matt. 5:38–48).

It is historical fact that God's Archenemy, the Devil, who started his rivalry-engagement against God from the creation of the world, is sowing the evil continuously in the hearts of humans. Let us browse the world history. We can find millions of tombs and monuments full of skeletons buried by wars of hatred, retaliation and revenge. Even today we hear and see such cruel and horrible violent and bloody conflicts being enacted in the name religious affiliation or political isms in countries like Ukraine, South Sudan, Nigeria, the Central African Republic, and in Syria. In this unending spiritual battle we can win only by the strategy Jesus handled in his own life: Forgiving and loving and praying for those victimized by the cruel Devil. He demonstrated it to us while he was hanging on the Cross. Pope Benedict emphasized this truth when he said once: "In fact, Christ's proposal is realistic because it takes into account that in the world there is too much violence, too much injustice, and therefore we can overcome this situation only countering it with more love, more kindness." However we should never think such a meek and forgiving style of life as surrender to the evil situations with sourgrape attitude or by an attitude of pacifism. Rather there is something more to this.

Certainly love for enemies seems madness to common reason and in the public square of post-modern society. On seeing so much evil in the world, especially when that evil affects us deeply, our reaction is always anger and perhaps revenge. But Jesus tells us not let evil force us to fight it with its own weapons of evil. He commands us to fight it with the weapons of God himself: mercy, forgiveness, even love of the evildoer and prayer for the ones who have hurt us.

In addition to the valid reasons the Divine and his sacred Writers have spelt out I would like to point out couple of reasons to forgive our enemies in human point of view: We, the humans, are very limited. We are weak, we are sick both physically and psychologically as well. No one is exempted in this regard. Though, as Paul writes in his Letter, we are the temple of the Holy Spirit, very easily we can destroy it and drive out the Good Spirit from our life. Besides, each one of us is a mystery who cannot be fully apprehended either by ourselves or by others. With these two human elements as backdrops we cannot easily, quickly and rightly judge other people's motivation or situation for their actions and reactions and even if we are sure of those things still we need to underscore the fact that the other is as weak and sick as we are.

I know many of us, as Catherine Marshall writes in her book *A Closer Walk* retort even to the Lord against his peculiar demand of forgetting the hurting deeds done by our neighbors. "My job was not finished, however. He told me, until I can forget what she has done. 'But how can I do that, Lord?' 'Your will is greater than your memory, Catherine. Rebuke the painful memory and cast it out in the name of Jesus.'" Once I heard the TV Evangelist Benny Hinn preaching about our human stupidity of never forgetting the hurts. As he said, most of us feel proud of our own self-effort of carrying with us the burden of hurt feelings even lifelong while Jesus requests us 'come to me all who are burdened and put the burdens down; I will carry them for you.'

Fr. James Martin wrote an article on "The Christian response to Bin Laden's Death" in an America magazine soon after Laden was killed. He ended his article as follows:

> Osama bin Laden was responsible for the murder of thousands of men and women in the United States, for the deaths and misery of millions across the world, and for the death of many servicemen and women, who made the supreme sacrifice of their lives. I am glad he has left the world. And I pray that his departure may lead to peace.

This is the Christian way, uniquely witnessing Jesus as our Savior, Lord and Master.

When we deeply analyze Jesus's hard-core demand of forgiving, forgetting the hurts but also praying for our offenders, we discover some remarkable backdrop behind this weird act. It is nothing but the 'life issue'. We, the committed followers of Jesus are not simply in favor of life for the unborn, for the innocent, for those we care for, for our families and friends, for our fellow citizens, for our fellow church members or even for those whom we consider good, but for all that are human. All life is sacred because God created all life; and because Christ died and resurrected for every human. When we hold a duty over respecting life-gift naturally we have to do the same for every human life breathing. This is why when we gather in the church for Sunday services we sing together a hymn 'Gather us in', composed by Marty Haugen, that spells out the beauty of variety and diversity of human lives assembled. We see in the church humans who are: the lost and forsaken, the blind and the lame, the young, the old who yearn for your face, the rich and the haughty, the proud and the strong. It is this weird but real "potpourri" of humanity for which Jesus shed his blood and wanted us to love, forgive and do good to all despite the differences.

Once again let us also remember what the Lord said at the end of his parable on the "unforgiving servant." "So will my heavenly Father do to you, unless each of you forgives your brother from your heart" (Matt. 18:35). Here we have to pay serious attention to his words: "From your heart." What he meant was, we need to forgive our enemies with human intelligence or reason but out of our will; to forgive out of sheer love; taking seriously Master Jesus's exhortation, Paul writes: "Owe no one anything, except to love one another; for the one who loves another has fulfilled the law" (Rom. 13:8). In addition Jesus expected our forgiveness of others to be total and not partial; not just once or twice or even seven times but with no count . . . "not seven times but seven-seventy times." Forgetting the sins of others indicates the totality of our forgiveness.

There is story about a Sage who went a riverbank to have a wash. He found there a scorpion struggling in water to get out. The sage pitied the scorpion and slowly took him by his hands from water. Suddenly the scorpion bit the sage. It hurt him and jumped again into the water. The sage went down again and tried to save him. But again and again the scorpion bit him and dropped himself into the water. The disciples of that sage were watching this scene very surprisingly and asked the sage why he was doing this as a crazy and insensible person. The sage replied to them: "My dear disciples! The scorpion behaved according to his nature and I acted in accordance with my nature. We the humans in order to become divine we have to forgive and help others." Yes indeed! To err is human but to forgive is divine.

The Post-Effects of Merciful Forgiveness

Forgiveness of other persons helps us to be healed. It is always a burden to carry grudges and resentment against our neighbors. It kills us first and then others. Mentally we become sick. As many psychiatric studies have proven, most of the sickness and illness in the body generate from the mental and psychological disturbances and hurts. Unless these roots are cleared off, the physical maladies and deceases cannot be cured. So this is one of the reasons why Jesus wants us to forgive others.

Benjamin A Vima

Surely our forgiveness heals others and binds our relationship once again. There are millions of people in this world, who maintain their relationship with their spouses, with their children, parents, and siblings and surely with the community members, will testify to this truth. Forgiveness has been the key element in keeping their relationship intact. There are many couples even before every sunset they remarry their spouses by forgiveness.

People in our lives hurt us because of believing rumors, gossips, long-standing prejudices, ignorance, sometimes out of good will and other times out of malice. In these circumstances what should we do? Go on brooding over? Continue to hurt ourselves, having recourse to isolation? Quit from our duties and responsibilities? Or Have we to retaliate or retort against evildoers? Have we to distance ourselves from their association or fellowship? This is what many of us plan to do and doing. What will happen is we may become more harm and pain to our neighbors, even our own friends! On the other hand if we forgive and forget others' hurting we will be privileged to play on our heavenly Father's lap!

While we speak about the positive effects of our total CHESED-based mercy-filled love toward our neighbors, we should also discuss a little bit of its negative and bitter effects. Our life is so much complicated. We are torn to pieces by our own getups, setups, dreams, ambitions, opportunities, ideas, philosophies, theologies, worldviews, cultures, colors, creeds, political parties, theories, discoveries, lab-tests, research studies and public opinions. We do not want to add one more to it in the form of too many dos and don'ts, commandments, rituals, rites, rubrics in religion. We like to take a simplistic way of leading life. Aware of our predicament, Jesus simplified the commandments Moses handed down to us into two:

> You shall love the Lord, your God, with all your heart, with all your soul, and with all your mind. This is the greatest and the first commandment. The second is like it: You shall love your neighbor as yourself. The whole law and the prophets depend on these two commandments. (Matt. 22:34–40)

Jesus's summary form of his religion sounds so good and pleasing to our ears. However when we dig into it and live by it in our daily lives we go through nightmares. Loving God is ok. Very simple and cozy to be out of the family, out of the street, pout of the town, out of the country and select a desert and live a monastic, isolated life and die. All I do there would be solely for expressing my total love for God. But that is not the complete summary of Jesus's religion. He adds to it a second one like the first, love my neighbors as myself. This means I should in no way leave my neighbors and my relationships with them.

After living in the midst of our neighbors, namely, parents, spouses, children, friends and relatives and other strange neighbors we should by now are well aware of the hard truth about the neighbors. A French philosopher, Jean Paul Sartre, exclaimed: Hell is nothing but our own neighbor. That is the reality. It is with them, through them, and in them we have to lead a life of love for God. Loving them as myself is a hard thing to do. This means as I accept myself with all my weaknesses, strengths, good and bad smells, sickness, health, inabilities, sinfulness, holiness sometimes, wrong and good choices and their prejudices and hypocrisies. This at least is tolerable; but Jesus asks us further a step to go with him and love these neighbors as he had loved us. Namely, to love even our enemies, to forgive them as he forgave and be ready to share everything of ourselves, including our very lives for them.

I always divide these two commandments as the first one directed to the irreligious people who have developed a tendency to stop with their love for human beings and the universe as philanthropists and humanitarian champions; and the second one is focused on the religious people who already find God as their sole proprietor and provider and destiny and love him totally. The first group forgets God but concentrates on neighbors and the second group while focusing their attention on God totally forget their neighbors.

We need to simplify our religion, but not too drastically like this. It is true by being faithful to both commandments of love we are torn between two loves. This is why any Christian who is sincere to his/her religion based on CHESED has to undergo such tension and terrible heartaches. If we pass through it, that is the 'narrow way' but the Highway of Jesus to win our victory.

CHAPTER 20

CHESED Action 4
Unhesitantly proclaiming the
CHESED Mercy of God

May God be gracious to us and bless us; may his face shine upon us. So shall your way be known upon the earth, your victory among all the nations! May the peoples praise you, God; may all the peoples praise you! (Ps. 67:2-4). This is the goal and content of every "merciful" disciple's proclamation which contains praising the Lord's marvelous deeds; his total victory of the universe; longing his Highway of justice, mercy and truth be known by all humans; consequently they too join with us proclaiming his CHESED as one family of God. As soon as we personally experience the marvels of God's CHESED we are expected by Jesus to proclaim it to others by words, deeds in truth and spirit and if need be, in blood. That is the 'testimony' Mary, Apostles, and all other disciples till this day have been giving as their primary purpose of life.

Now let us discuss about the ways of accomplishing this splendid act of proclamation as the mercy-filled disciple of Jesus.

Proclaiming God's **CHESED** in Solitude

An entrepreneur noted for his ruthlessness in his pursuit of success visited Mark Twain, the famous writer: Before I die, I vow that I will travel to Mount Sinai, climb to the top and read aloud the Ten Commandments. Twain replied, I have a better idea; you could stay home in Boston and learn to keep them. Before we become merciful, charitable, lovable, sharing and caring the others in public first and foremost let us turn to God in Jesus first in confessing (proclaiming) to him our gratitude toward his continuous mercy showered to us.

We read in Luke, Mary, Mother of Jesus, kept all these things (the CHESED actions of God), reflecting on them in her heart (2: 19). This is what first and foremost every 'mercy-experienced' person would do. The unceasing prayer of the 'merciful' persons to gain their 'blessedness', must be one of a servant who is always faithful, vigilant, and focusing attention only to the moves of the Master and such a prayer surely would proclaim the greatness of the Master who has bestowed them chances to fulfill his CHESED-performance through their hands. They should begin, proceed and end their life's undertakings and accomplishments with the heartfelt prayer the Church prays in one of her Morning Liturgy of the Hour Prayers: Lord our God, give us grace to serve you always with joy, because our full and lasting happiness is to make of our lives a constant service to the Author of all that is good. In addition to it, at the end of the day burdened with responsibilities and hectic roles as family members, church members, and ordinary citizens, the merciful would be recited what their Master taught them: "We are unprofitable servants; we have done what we were obliged to do" (Luke 17:10).

When we proclaim God's CHESED privately and personally God is very much pleased with us. And Jesus his Son too encouraged us so. When you pray, he said, go to your inner room, close the door, and pray to your Father in secret. And your Father who sees in secret will repay you. He meant that when we pray we should be very personal with God, paying full attention to him and intimately communicate to him. This is the reason he made us call God "Abba" a more warmly term than "Father." Jesus too expected us to hold a person-to-person contact with him. To emphasize his desire he looked for such transaction from his disciples and from those who benefitted from his healing mercy. The best example for this truth is found in a healing event Luke narrates in his Gospel. It is about Jesus's merciful cure of ten lepers (Luke 17:11-19). When ten lepers had been bestowed the gift of healing of their leprosy, only one of them returned, glorifying God in a loud voice and he fell at the feet of Jesus and thanked him. Jesus expressed his feelings of disappointment and hurt at noticing the ungrateful nine healed lepers' ungrateful attitude, nonetheless he appreciated the one who came in person to express his sentiments of thanks. He admired at the thankful healed man who did a very personal proclamation of his personal feelings of faith in Jesus's greatness and his CHESED.

The true merciful people are to be conscious of Jesus's redemptive power as the divine healer. Out of his CHESED-based mercy he intervened in our lives especially in our moments of pain. We observe in him the CHESED deeds of the Triune God who brought to us repeated forgiveness and the capacity to forgive and to love. Among all God's blessings shared with us through Jesus the greatest are amazing grace, justifiable salvation, immense mercy, and unthinkable holiness. As mercy-filled persons sometimes we admire at our superb personality. But if we stop and think deeply the blessed life we inherited is not what we have, but who we have become, in and through Jesus Christ. Through his gracious benevolence all of us, who were born in sin and lived in darkness as no-people, became God's people, his friends and disciples by being reborn in Jesus's Chesed.

Undoubtedly most of us still lead a life of in and out frequently and even steadily I mean drifting away the returning back to the fold of Jesus by getting his wonderful forgiveness. Thanks to his love we share some of his Chesed deeds to the needy and the sick. He grants some of us to experiencing a blessed life by casting into the deep, that means 'going beyond' what others cannot tread in, following the Lord to a life of radical and blessed missionary discipleship. It is for this we should daily do to him the proclamation of gratitude and faithfulness. "Life without thankfulness is devoid of love and passion. Hope without thankfulness is lacking in fine perception. Faith without thankfulness lacks strength and fortitude. Every virtue divorced from thankfulness is maimed and limps along the spiritual road" (John Henry Jowett).

In connection to what we considered above, I would like to add here a historical statement of George Washington, a God-fearing President of the United States about his thoughts on thanking the Lord. On Oct. 3,

1789, George Washington, recommending and assigning Thursday the 26th day of November as the annual Thanksgiving Day, wrote in his Letter: This day is to be devoted by the People of these States to the service of that great and glorious Being, who is the beneficent Author of all the good that was, that is, or that will be. That we may then all unite in rendering unto him our sincere and humble thanks—for his kind care and protection of the People of this Country previous to their becoming a Nation—for the signal and manifold mercies, and the favorable interpositions of his Providence which we experience in the course and conclusion of the late war . . . and in general for all the great and various favors which he hath been pleased to confer upon us. It was a most striking testimony for how the great persons in history uphold their sense of gratitude to their Creator and turn out to be the "real heroes."

This personal and direct proclamation to the Triune God has been one of daily chores in the lives of prophets, sages and saints. We, the "merciful" who are promised "blessedness" should follow their footsteps in this regard. With Prophet Isaiah, our hearts and lips must be continuously thanking and praising the Creator and his Son for their marvelous deeds in our midst. And you will say on that day: give thanks to the LORD, acclaim his name; among the nations make known his deeds, proclaim how exalted is his name. Sing praise to the LORD for he has done glorious things; let this be known throughout all the earth. Shout with exultation, City of Zion, for great in your midst is the Holy One of Israel! (12:4–6).

We should be never tired of singing and proclaiming the CHESED of God as David does in his Psalms.

201

Consistently we discover this act of proclamation in most of his Psalms. He starts Ps. 101 with joyful-signing of God's CHESED: I sing of mercy and justice; to you, LORD, I sing praise. (NABRE); I will sing of chesed and mishpat; unto Thee, Hashem, will I sing. (OJB) In some other Psalms like 51 while he confesses to the Lord his sinfulness loudly and consciously, and pleading for God's merciful treatment toward him, he too includes some promises as amendment and penance for his misdeeds. He promises that he would start teaching others to come out of their sins; that he will go on proclaiming God's Chesed; and he will continue offering his contrite spirit as pleasing sacrifice to the Lord.

In the Gospel of Luke (1:46–45), we read Mary, Mother of Jesus, sang an unforgettable song of praise and gratitude when she encountered the Holy One's CHESED in hers and her people's lives as well. She starts the canticle saying: My soul proclaims the greatness of the Lord; my spirit rejoices in God my savior. (46-47) Then she proceeds to list out the marvelous CHESED-deeds of God as the source of her joy. She confesses that God's mercy has been lasting forever (50). She underlines how God's justice and mercy played the historical roles both of overturning the history of evil humans and of uplifting his anawim (51-54); and she ends her song with an emphasis on how God did all those deeds according to his covenantal promises (55).

Mary's canticle of praise has been an example all her Son's disciples in proclaiming God's CHESED in their daily life. One thing we should remember here. Luke purposely placed Mary's canticle of CHESED not only after she was personally blessed by the Creator with a heavenly Baby but also after her deeds of mercy to her cousin Elizabeth and her baby John in her womb (ref. Luke 1:39–45). As representative of God and moved by God's Spirit, Elizabeth offered three blessings to Mary: Most blessed are you among women, and blessed is the fruit of your womb . . . Blessed are you who believed that what was spoken to you by the Lord would be fulfilled. The CHESED-proclamation cannot occur simply in any ordinary humans; and certainly not in the humans who are merciless, cold, unjust and unfaithful. It is possible only from the hearts of the 'the blessed merciful' as Jesus's Mother. They only know the inner dwelling of CHESED and its external manifestations. The blessed merciful persons proclaim God's CHESED at every moment of their life and at every step they take for their and others' development. As Paul insists, they would be proclaiming God's CHESED not only through praying unceasingly and in all circumstances (1 Thess. 5:17–18).

Proclaiming God's CHESED in Public

God through Jesus wants us to proclaim his saving endeavors to the entire world. When Jesus was ready to return to his Father, he entrusted to his disciples a grand commission of offering the entire humanity God's merciful forgiveness and directed them to preach and teach about the values he brought to this world (Ref. Matt. 28:18–20; John 20:21–23; Luke 24:46–49). Hence, Apostles like Paul did and advised all his disciples to be proclaiming the Gospel of mercy through preaching and teaching in season and out of season (2 Tim. 4:2).

Our public proclamation of the God's CHESED should be the kind of angels' proclamation portrayed in the book of Revelation (7:11–12). All the angels stood around the throne and around the elders and the four living creatures. They prostrated themselves before the throne, worshiped God, and exclaimed, "Victory to our God, who sits on the throne, and to the Lamb! Praise and glory and wisdom and thanksgiving and honor and power and strength to our God for ever and ever. Amen."

We notice almost all the people who were healed by the merciful deeds of Jesus are said not only to join his team but also to walk around their neighborhood and nook and corner of their villages and cities proclaimed and testified to what the mercy of Jesus has done for them. Let me list out a few: The man who was healed of his leprosy, by the merciful hands of Jesus, was so excited and being urged by his faith and gratitude went out and began spreading the healing news, even though Jesus admonished him not to tell anyone. Also the healed person didn't attempt to fulfill his religio-social law to perform some healing rituals. His only preoccupation was to tell the good news of Jesus healing him. Mark writes at the end of this event narration: The man went away and began to publicize the whole matter. He spread the report abroad so that it was impossible for Jesus to enter a town openly. He remained outside in deserted places, and people kept coming to him from everywhere (Mark 1:40–45).

Once Jesus healed two blind men by touching their eyes. As soon as they got cured, they were urged from the bottom of their hearts to proclaim merciful Jesus's name. Once again we observe the healed persons were so thrilled by awe and surely overwhelmed by their thankfulness, that they didn't even hear what Jesus was saying to them. Mark writes: And their eyes were opened. Jesus warned them sternly, "See that no one knows about this." But they went out and spread word of him through all that land (Matt. 9:27-31). In another healing event when Jesus cured a deaf man brought by the public, Mark describes about the reaction of the public. Especially those who brought the deaf to Jesus and saw directly the mercy-filled healing were so stirred up that not paying attention to Jesus's admonition, they began proclaiming the mercy of Jesus. He ordered them not to tell anyone. But the more he ordered them not to, the more they proclaimed it. They were exceedingly astonished and they said, "He has done all things well. He makes the deaf hear and [the] mute speak" (Mark 7: 31-37).

When any proclamation about Jesus comes from the deep faith and gratitude to him, it cannot be obstructed by any humans-even they possess power, money and so on. That is what we notice in John's narration about the healing of man born blind. His experience of Jesus's merciful healing brought him to an audacious conviction that his healer couldn't but be a prophet. He started proclaiming it to whomsoever questioning him. John underlines this faith-filled attitude of the healed man by quoting his answer to the hierarchy: "You hold on to any judgment about my healer; I don't care; but he then added a historical statement: One thing I do know is that I was blind and now I see" (John 9:1-38).

Proclaiming God's CHESED by Our Joy

The great French novelist Leon Bloy said, "Joy is the most infallible sign of the presence of God." The joy in question is not necessarily a bubbly feeling. In the ancient world, they understood happiness differently than we do today. For Aristotle, happiness referred not so much to a passing emotion as to a whole quality of life: being in a right relationship with other human beings, with the world and ultimately with God. One of the lines in Beethoven's "Ode to Joy" says, "Even a worm has contentment." That is, the lowly worm is in correct relationship with its world. For the worm it comes naturally. For us, we need to work at it—and to receive help from above.

Unquestionably the Christian joy that sparkles in our eyes, on the face from the bottom of our heart is the most striking proclamation of our experience of God's CHESED. There are many symbols and signs to depict what Christianity is. Among them the most influential sign is the smiling face of a Christian. Late Archbishop Oscar Romero in his first pastoral letter emphasized the need for Christians to be joyful: "It is wrong to be sad. Christians cannot be pessimists; Christians must always nourish in their hearts the fullness of joy. William Barclay echoes the same sentiment as he says: "A gloomy Christian is contradiction in terms."

Whatever we do in the name of Jesus's Gospel, it should be based on its core kerygma of joy. That is the first heavenly message proclaimed by an angel to the shepherds: "Do not be afraid; for behold, I proclaim to you good news of great joy that will be for all the people (Luke 2:9-10). In sharing this gift of Godly joy, as Paul VI wrote in his Apostolic Exhortation Gaudete in Domino (9 May 1975), 22: AAS 67 (1975), 297.5), no one is excluded from the joy brought by the Lord.

We firmly believe that this joy is dwelling in all persons who try to encounter Jesus in their lives. It is achieved by any Christian disciple only by an experiential life with God in Jesus. Pope Francis, introducing his apostolic exhortation Evangelii Gaudium, wrote: The joy of the gospel fills the hearts and lives of all who encounter Jesus. Those who accept his offer of salvation are set free from sin, sorrow, inner emptiness and loneliness. With Christ joy is constantly born anew. In this Exhortation I wish to encourage the Christian faithful to embark upon a new chapter of evangelization marked by this joy, while pointing out new paths for the Church's journey in years to come.

The true encounter of this Gospel joy of Jesus has been from the beginning of God's economy of salvation. Sacred Writers in the Bible pinpoint the real reason and source of this fact of rejoicing. Certainly it is because of our faith that our God in Jesus esteems us as his fiancé and adorned us with so many blessings as Isaiah paraphrased it: He has clothed me with garments of salvation, and wrapped me in a robe of justice, like a bridegroom adorned with a diadem, as a bride adorns herself with her jewels (Isa. 61:10). With Isaiah we go little further and contend with him the most hilarious reason for our joy. We claim that each one of us is not mere fiancé to God; rather we are his spouses. God has revealed to us that the heavenly wedding had already taken place between God and ourselves. For as a young man marries a virgin, your Builder shall marry you; And as a bridegroom rejoices in his bride so shall your God rejoice in you (Isa. 62:5).

With Hannah, Samuel's mother, who proclaimed her joy as she related it to God's victory in her private and family life, we too feel the same sense of joy at our Lord's merciful deeds of saving us from both spiritual and temporal perils, saying: My heart exults in the LORD, my horn is exalted by my God. I have swallowed up my enemies; I rejoice in your victory (1 Sam. 1). Undoubtedly by the awareness of our sins forgiven by the amazing grace of God in Jesus we are so overwhelmed with joy and sing joyful hymns with David. Just one sample from his Psalms. He begins Psalm 32 singing, blessed is the one whose fault is removed, whose sin is forgiven, continues it with his proclamation of how God's forgiveness liberated him from distress and filled him with joy, singing, you guard me from distress; with joyful shouts of deliverance you surround me and ends it with an invitation to others who have been acquitted by God like him, singing Be glad in the LORD and rejoice, you righteous; exult, all you upright of heart (Ps. 32).

The same experience of God's CHESED-deeds in our lives and in others too fills us with astounding joy as that of Mary, Mother of Jesus, whose Canticle has proven this: "My spirit rejoices in God my Savior, for he has looked upon his lowly servant." Apostle Paul is not exhausted in encouraging us to rejoice always. We agree with his valid reasons why we should be in such a hilarious attitude. First we believe that this is the will of God for us in Christ Jesus; second, the one who calls us is faithful, and he will also accomplish it; third, God, who is rich in mercy, because of the great love he had for us, even when we were dead in our transgressions, brought us to life with Christ.

When John the Baptizer announced Jesus's coming in our midst, he testified to his encountering the joy Jesus brought with him. Even while he was in the womb of his mother Elizabeth, John expressed his joy at Infant Jesus's presence in Mary's womb. At the moment the sound of your greeting reached my ears, the infant in my womb leaped for joy (Luke 1:44). Plus, his joy came from his genuine humility of identifying himself as a messenger, a witness, a forerunner, a humble herald, and a friend to the Bridegroom. You yourselves can testify that I said [that] I am not the Messiah, but that I was sent before him. The one who has the bride is the bridegroom; the best man, who stands and listens to him, rejoices greatly at the bridegroom's voice. So this joy of mine has been made complete (John 3:28-29).

In Jesus's physical absence let us act as Jesus by making others joyful. The poor were Jesus's great concern. We are disciples of Jesus. How much do we reach out to the poor like him? How many poor are there still among us? While we make the poor and the needy joyful, our joy is doubled; while they see Jesus the Messiah in our good works, we will be confirmed in hope, patience and faith. It is a joy of living and acting as Jesus in disguise. It is a joy of sharing and sacrificing for the uplifting of the poor, the sick and the needy. We try our best to move and work within the enlightened territory of God; however we should never think there will be no problems and hurdles. They are part and parcel of our stewardship. As one leader of modern time said, "we will have people who don't like what we do, but we better have our own vision, and we better have our own will and our own passion and determination; holding always in mind that now the life requires work and sacrifice and sometimes it's painful, but there is a lot of joy and there is a lot of hope and possibility."

The Psalmist prays in Psalm 92, 'Lord we proclaim your love in the morning, and your faithfulness in the night.' That should be our attitude toward our life. Our life's cycle consists of day and night, brightness and darkness, ups and downs, spring and fall, summer and winter. When we face with the bright daytime of life we should proclaim God's love and mercy by performing Love-deeds to other people, by sharing the produces, the talents, the savings, and go out of the way, out of the family, out of the self-centric campus and extend our loving hands to the needy to express our love for God. Also when we are encircled by the darkness of life, the night of our soul, we should in no way get weary, cold, and indifferent and stop performing the love deeds. On those gloomy days we have to witness to the fidelity of the Lord. In other words, not losing hope or faith in his love and goodness, we should continue to be firm in love-walk and in our joyful expression of love to God through worship and prayer.

For many humans the joyful Christmas day is once a year; but for us the merciful disciples every day is Christmas day; liturgically we may celebrate one Sunday of Advent as 'Laetare Sunday' a 'rejoicing Sunday', for us who want to be called by Jesus 'the blessed', every day is 'Laetare Day' a rejoicing Day; Every day we are seriously but joyfully and hopefully waiting for the full revelation of God in Jesus as an expectant mother. Every day therefore is a sort of 'a day of Shower'. The only difference here is the expectant mother on her day of shower is presented by her relatives and friends with their gifts of love and appreciation and thus make her happier; but in our case, we, who are hopefully expecting Jesus's glorious coming, go to those around us who are more earnestly expecting Jesus to come and bestow their food, dress, shelter and surely love and peace and joy, and share with them the blessings Jesus already has filled us with. By our smile, by our love and concern, we make their day happier and fulfilling and start with us seeking the fullness of life Jesus only can offer.

Pope Francis from the onset of his pontificate longs the entire church derives its whole identity from its mission to preach the gospel and to do so joyfully. This means in particular those of us who strive to be 'the merciful' as our Master should understand ourselves as missionaries who are called to share God's mercy with a suffering world with joy and not like 'sourpusses' who proclaim knowingly or unknowingly about "tomb psychology." His spirit reminds us of a remarkable maxim of Saint Francis de Sales: A sad saint is a sorry saint.

Proclaiming God's **CHESED** through Deeds

Though we would be elaborately treat this subject in next chapter, let us speak about the inner drive with which the 'merciful' would accomplish their mercy-deeds. In the first chapter of his section we treated about the aim, goal and incentive of all our merciful deeds including what said in previous chapters. While all of them were related to our personal lives, here we would be dealing exclusively with those mercy-deeds performed to others.

As we read in Luke the woman who got her sins forgiven joint then with the team of women who accompanied Jesus in his journey of preaching and proclaiming the good news around Palestine. Besides we are told that they became helpers and supporters of Jesus's Messianic Ministries with all their might. I think most of Jesus's wellwishers and cooperators in his redemptive ministry were those who have been already healed by him both in body and soul. Hence as Paul insists, the love of Christ urged them to be lovers of the needy and the poor.

According to his conviction, all merciful servants should act as though they have been liberated. This is what we are underlining in this chapter. Church prays earnestly in her Divine Office (Advent Morning Prayer) that as we proclaim your saving power to others, let us not ourselves lose hold of your salvation. Let us now go forward knowing what we should do concretely to the afflicted and the needy and pledge to accomplish them so that we with our beneficiaries may live our lives to the full in this world and transfigure it with the hope of future glory.

CHAPTER 21

Chesed Action 5
Empowered by the Spirit Doing
Spiritual Acts of Mercy

Reminder of the Ultimate Goals of Merciful Acts

A s we have elaborately discussed about the spirit behind
the acts of mercy and the goals to be envisioned by us
while performing such charitable deeds, now let's straight
away go to list out those merciful acts the disciples of
Jesus are obliged to carry out in daily life. Before going in
details of the list of merciful acts, let us remind ourselves
the twofold ultimate reason for which we strenuously
perform our all acts of mercy, especially the spiritual ones.
It is not only for the forgiveness of our personal sins but
also for the salvation of the beneficiaries. Peter writes in
his Letter: Above all, let your love for one another be
intense, because love covers a multitude of sins (1 Pet. 4:8).
Expounding the proverb Peter quoted from OT, James
tells us: . . . whoever brings back a sinner from the error
of his way will save his soul from death and will cover a

multitude of sins (James 5:20). Saint Vincent de Paul well said: Extend your mercy towards others, so that there can be no one in need whom you meet without helping. For what hope is there for us if God should withdraw His Mercy from us?

Traditionally the Church admonishes us to perform our merciful acts under two categories: 1. Spiritual Acts. 2. Corporal (bodily) Acts. Saint Augustine dreamt of the results of these two acts as the two works of mercy set a person free.

Spiritual Acts of Mercy

When God in Jesus speaks about human poverty he always portrays its twofoldness: The material and spiritual poverty. Every human at one time or another is affected by either of these two poverties. The more serious poverty of the two is spiritual poverty because it depletes all our peace, joy, and sense of purpose in life; besides it is a sort of inner pest that can last forever. It is this poverty Jesus the Good Samaritan targeted to fill in, to heal and to obliterate from our soul. When Jesus and the Prophets and the Disciples teach about "bring poor in spirit" they point out "being spiritually poor." It means a person's feeling of utter spiritual bankruptcy before God; understanding oneself absolutely nothing of worth to offer God; admitting oneself completely destitute spiritually and one's inability to deliver one's self from one's dreadful situation of sin.

Moreover we earlier exposed that such kind of poverty in spirit is very much appreciated by God and Jesus as the most valuable and fruitful anawim spirit. The problem is most of the humanity, not considering this life situation as a frightful crisis, don't try to take either precaution or cure. Consequently this spiritual poverty turns out to be in-depth spiritual sickness, gets soared and brings in various maladies to the psychological, intellectual, and physical dimensions of humans. At this moment, the human spirit craves for the nourishment of truth, goodness, balance, and beauty if it is to be healthy and accomplish what it has been created for before death. The spiritual acts of mercy which God through Jesus and the Church recommends to us are meant to be preventive and curative medical treatments and medicines.

Jesus's primary act of mercy was splendidly prophesied by Isaiah which Jesus himself confirmed it (Luke 4:21) at his first public address in a synagogue:

> The spirit of the Lord GOD is upon me, because the LORD has anointed me; he has sent me to bring good news to the afflicted, to bind up the brokenhearted, to proclaim liberty to the captives, release to the prisoners, to announce a year of favor from the LORD and a day of vindication by our God; to comfort all who mourn; to place on those who mourn in Zion a diadem instead of ashes, to give them oil of gladness instead of mourning, a glorious mantle instead of a faint spirit. (Isa. 61: 1–3)

In the light of this heavenly manifesto for the spiritual deeds of "merciful," the Church formulates seven Spiritual Acts: First of all like Jesus the Anointed, the merciful should "bring good news to the afflicted"; "proclaim liberty to and release those who are bound and captured by evils"; and "announce the year of favor from the Lord and a day of vindication by our God." These three acts are capsuled by the Church's first three formulated spiritual acts of mercy: (1) admonish sinners, (2) instruct the uninformed, and (3) counsel the doubtful. Jesus's other spiritual acts of mercy are "to bind up the brokenhearted" and "to comfort all who mourn," which are catechized by the Church through the other four spiritual acts of mercy: (4) comfort the sorrowful, (5) be patient with those in error, (6) forgive offenses, and (7) pray for the living and the dead.

Among these Spiritual Acts, admonishing sinners, instructing the uninformed, counseling the doubtful, being patient with those in error and forgiving offenses have been treated in details in previous chapters. Nonetheless I would like to add a few more points in this regard.

Admonishing sinners, instructing the uninformed, and counseling the doubtful, are the hardest acts in this postmodern society. A few days before I began writing this chapter one of friends asked the difference between autobiography and biography; he knew both are about the lives of humans. But he didn't know about their publication deals. I explained to him the real difference. In our conversation I bypassed the subject and commented that all of us born and grown in this world leave behind after death, a living bible of our own; I too added that though all Christians have, hold and read and follow a 'common Bible' all individually write our personal bible in which we fill in the events, words, anecdotes, experiences, and surely upholdings, values and accomplishments relatively different from another individual's. Even though we don't publish our bibles as biographies or autobiographies, our posterity will inherit our bibles either in blood, or in memory or in vogue and gossip.

This is the problem with the modern people. We know what our life is; what our weakness and strength is; what our worthiness and worthlessness is. We don't need any body to come and impose their ideas, their values and their judgements. We live in a culture of "I-am-okay-and you-are-okay" or "you-may-not be okay." As I hold the Bible of my own values and others have their own personal Bible of values. You respect my territory as I do yours. This sort of far-fetched 'golden rule' empowers every modern mind. In this extreme utopian cultural environment we would become most unpopular by performing any sort of spiritual acts like admonishing, counseling or instructing. Unquestionably it is not stress-free to perform spiritual acts of mercy among the new generation. It takes chivalrous attitude of faith, hope and charity, wisdom from God's Spirit to find right moment and right words in this venture. This is why our Master exhorts us, the merciful, to perform such acts but with discretion, about which we have discussed well in the previous chapter on "Forgive others."

One thing we need to remember in this spiritual endeavor is what Paul states, not only out of the revelation he received from his crucified Master' but also from his own personal experiences of doing these acts of mercy. Namely we should first avoid by all means any human trickeries and deceitful schemes; but live the truth in love and then perform these hardest acts of mercy. He too advises us, as we try to lead a life renewed in God's way in righteousness and holiness of truth, we should be cautiously dealing with the hardhearted, licentious, impure and callous generation of our time; and shunning bitterness, fury, anger, shouting, and reviling along with all malice, we should be kind to one another, compassionate, forgiving one another as God has forgiven you in Christ (Eph. 4:14–32). Such a kind of move psychologically and surely inspirationally brings to effect what is expected of those spiritual acts of mercy.

Let us now talk about the two other spiritual acts: comforting the sorrowful and praying for the living and the dead.

Comforting the Sorrowful

The term *comfort* comes from the Latin root word *cum-fortis*, meaning "with strength." Etymologically therefore to comfort indicates to strengthen someone. In this way, when we apply it to the act of mercy 'comfort the sorrowful' or 'comfort the afflicted' it clearly states the merciful, through performing this act of mercy to the sorrowful restores the sorrowful to their strength; enables them to persevere and to summon them to the courage that strongly resists those who would seek to render him weak or ineffective.

Every baby born in this world is simply a bundle of few pounds of flesh and bones. Added to it there is certain electric power that runs through head to foot. Undoubtedly a few percentage in humanity are born physically challenged as the blind, the mute, the deaf, and the dumb and so on. However the truthful fact is every human in one way or another born handicapped emotionally, intellectually and spiritually. As Christians we uphold that except Mary and John the Baptizer, all of us are born spiritually handicapped. Paul writes about this in metaphorical way: For you were once darkness, but now you are light in the Lord (Eph. 5:8).

To come out of emotional and intellectual disability we help each other as family, friends and society in the form of counseling, advice and education. But regarding our spiritual debility only God, the supreme Spirit, can deal. We are spiritually blind to know, to love and to serve our God as Creator and Redeemer. Many of us chronically blind in our sinfulness to be conscious of God's active presence in and around our lives; others are hardheartedly deaf to listen to God's voice; many others are dumb and mute to proclaim God's marvelous deeds in our midst. There are too many among us grown spiritually empty, judgmental, envious, suspicious, afraid, autonomous, depressed, lonely, disconnected, and out of energy.

Surprisingly even after so many global researches have been undertaken on the above-mentioned precarious life-situation of humanity and all the more so after encountering such deplorable conditions of human life majority in human society are not fully conscious of it and behaving cold and complacent toward it. In this modern world there are two groups of spiritually handicapped people: While on one side of the world where poverty and ignorance dominate people and they grope in darkness, being blind in superstitious practices and even turn out to be religious terrorists; on the other side we notice so many being blind of the presence of God and the need of connections with him in faith, hope and love. Blindness of not seeing the meaning of human life, its goal, its destiny and its power makes many of us dislike religion, especially the organized religions, religious and spiritual practices.

Keeping what we discussed above as the backdrop or base we are pained to observe so many around us are spiritually sick, mentally irrational, and also physically ill of many kinds. They are continuously shedding tears, being sorrowful about their wretched situation. Human life is filled with so many crises in the form of sufferings, problems and other odds of life. In OT we hear about the 'sorrowful Job'. At his momentous life-crisis he considered human life is very unfair and it is drudgery. Therefore he cried out: "I am filled with restlessness until the dawn. My days are swifter than a weaver's shuttle; they come to an end without hope." With the loss of hope he utters: "My life is like the wind; I shall not see happiness again." As a matter of fact Job's words are echoing our own today's mourning. Our world is full of suffering and pain; many people are in agony and distress and are victims of exploitation and injustice. As the Psalmist declares, we are all broken hearted, being tossed by too many anxieties.

These human sufferings can be categorized into two groups: The crises of nagging and hurting mental agony, psychological traumas and other interior sufferings based on anxieties, tensions, sleepless nights and many other disappointment-feelings. These sufferings can be categorized as the primary group. The second group is the numerous physical sicknesses, people's rejections, our failures, others' infidelity and the worst of all is our death. If we read the entire Book of Job we can discover all these crises had affected Job's life. That is the sorrowful story of Job and surely of many of our fellowmen mourning and groaning.

It is to them our Master wants us to reach out our merciful hands. Being already wounded by the same or worse situation as others experience but fortunately helped and healed by God and his agents, we now are commanded to go as 'wounded healers' like Jesus in helping out the sorrowful.

There are too many breaking incidents happening in and around human lives. Life breaks us open and hollows us out. A loved one dies; an illness strikes; a relationship ends. They become truly break-points. A breakpoint is a point in life where something stops, pauses, changes, or breaks apart, such as heart-breaking, family-breaking, job breaking, which are consequently supposed to become source of turning-point, defining moment decision point in our life's journey. Regrettably not all profit like this; rather they are torn to pieces and sadly make recourse to perverted actions. We the merciful must go after these people as Good Samaritan do our best in pouring on their hearts the oil of gladness and healing.

Pope Francis never fails repeating his main thought about the Church and calls it 'field-hospital'. In one of his daily homilies, pointing out those who were in pews he was quoted saying, there are many "wounded" waiting in the aisles of the Church for a minister of Christ to heal them from their pains and sorrows and liberate them from the demons that plague them. These wounded people may be in our homes, neighborhoods, and in and around the globe. He too added, that Jesus has been a wounded healer. Following him we should say, even in our troubles, "Let us go on to the nearby villages that I may preach there also. For this purpose have I come."

In that Pope's spirit, I had been consistent in preaching not only to myself in prayertime but also to my parishioners that we should never to be either couchpotatos, or ruminating and eating our own pains and sorrows or with sourgrape attitude stop extending our helping hands beyond personal family, friends and racial subgroups. We must be ready to go beyond our likes and dislikes. That is the only way for a Christian to be a merrygoer and a jollygoodfellow even in pains, sufferings and perils.

A man came to me one day to have some sort of counseling. He began to share some of his life's experiences. He said that he attempted many times suicide many years he had lost faith in God, in religion, in rituals, in others, in the world, above all in his very life. He had felt that he was wasting his life with no results. He found himself useless and trash. So he even made attempts to kill himself. But one day one of his neighbors approached him with great concern and love. With her she also brought him a plate of good delicious dinner. As he was eating his sumptuous meal his friend did not speak much to him but listened to him and uttered a few words like 'I fully trust you.' My client told me those few words of that friend changed his entire life. 'She trusted me, father,' he said, 'I felt I had at least one person in the world who trusted me and so I must live to prove it.' The beautiful lessen I got from this anecdote narrated to me by one of my mentors was that more than the delicious food and other material helps (though they too can be instrumental) as the Good Samaritan's two silver coins given to the innkeeper (Ref. Luke 10:35) the friendly Christian trust communicated to my clients of mercy would bring the end results Jesus longs for. Father George Kosicki, CSB, the great Divine Mercy evangelist, once summed up the meaning of this Latin word as follows: misericordia means "having a pain in your heart for the pains of others, and taking pains to do something about their pain."

Hence, of all the spiritual works of mercy, comforting the sorrowful requires the greatest patience, sensitivity, and also silence. I learned this factor when I underwent a course on 'Hospital Chaplaincy'. My professor, besides demonstrating this truth by his own dealings in our visiting the sick, pointed out to us the Scriptural and psychological elements contained in treating human grief. He told us that sorrow or grief often has a life and logic of its own; often it must be allowed to run its course. Grief is something we can rarely get around; we must simply go through it. Thus, comforting or consoling the sorrowful and grieving people in our life often involves a kind of silent and understanding accompaniment more so than words or actions. He finally said, 'to listen and give understanding attention often provides the greatest value.'

I began to put his teaching into practice. Though preachy as I am I found it hard in the beginning; later I enjoyed it because I discovered soon that greater relief and peace I shared with the sorrowful by my loving listening to them or by friendly gestures of grasping hands together, hugging and laying my healing hands on them than wordy discussions. I too started believing that a largely silent and respectful silence can be a way of honoring grief and signaling a true fellowship. The wise Apostle Paul writes, "Weep with those who weep" (Rom 12:15). Though it may sound strange, I love one online writer recommending us in this act of mercy to follow the dogs. It is true when we have a bad day, the best thing our dog does is it just sits close by and nuzzles us gently. May be that's a down-to-earth 'doggy' model.

My instructor on grief-ministry also advised me that if I notice a sorrowful person getting "stuck" in his/her grief, not making the progress of moving through it in stages, I should understand that person needs more time and room. During those hours/days I require greater sensitivity to discover what the sorrowful person needs; and that should be not on our terms but his/her. If I feel failing in my attempts of mercy-filled comforting, I was told to sort more professional help that person.

In this connection, I desire to caution my readers regarding the major difference between psychotherapeutic treatment and our spiritual act of mercy. As one Catholic Psychologist points out, in psychotherapy there is no direct referencing or appeal to God's mystery, protection, providence, mercy, or forgiveness while the spiritual works of mercy are much richer than psychotherapy and more efficacious. In contrast to the natural humanistic endeavor found in psychotherapy of 'mere human companionship', in the act of mercy three persons-God, the counselor and counselee meet together in the spiritual realm.

A unanimous writer posted a poetic appeal of a grieving person which I perceive the voice of the sorrowful people around me: 'When I am trodden down, come hold my hand; when I am weary lost to life and when hours pass from day to night, come hold my hand and sing to me a song so low in quiet stirrings; do not let go, come hold my hand!'

Finally this is what I want to testify: Whenever I am wearied in accomplishing this toughest act of mercy I never forget to sing within my heart: Since we are summoned to a silent place; struggling to find the words to fill the space. Christ be beside us as we grieve; daring to doubt or to believe.

Praying for the Living and the Dead

Among the ingredients of "qualityprayer" which I have dealt with in my book 'Prayerfully Yours', placing our petitions to the Lord in faith, hope and confidence is one. The title Church uses here for the seventh spiritual act of mercy may seem projecting only that kind of intercession and petition. But if we go deeper into its spirit we discover some more spiritual matters contained in it.

First one is that whatever we perform in the name of Jesus's mercy must be consecrated by his merciful heart. This is why Saint Faustina exhorts us to offer all our merciful acts to the bountiful divine mercy of Jesus. The true Catholic Christian spirituality, as I have pointed out in my book *Catholic Christian Spirituality for New Age Dummies*, demands that all that we think, speak and act must be done in, through and with and for Jesus. Otherwise all our performances would be futile as mere humanitarian and philanthropic undertakings and will not bear solid fruits.

Secondly when we begin to pray for the benefits of the living and the dead our prayer should include our craving and demanding of the Spirit's power from on High so that in every step we take into the mercy-field may become effective and efficient. Thirdly the intercession for the living and the dead becomes an element of communicating to God both our inability and his omnipotent miraculous power. Our works of mercy, both corporal and spiritual, will always appear inadequate compared to the needs of the world around us. However we should never be disheartened; on the contrary we kneel down to God and showing what we plan to do, how little we are capable of accomplishing and pledge to abide in him with trust, hope and confidence. We too express our waiting for his marvelous mercy deeds through us.

All preachers expound this remarkable aptitude of every disciple of Jesus as 'the merciful', when they interpret the Gospel event of multiplication of loaves (John 6:1–15). When the Lord planned to feed more than 5000 hungry stomachs, he directed his Apostles to bring to him whatever food was available around that area. Even though his disciples pointed out the meagerness of the available food-five barley loaves and two fish, compared to the ample need-even two hundred days' wages worth of food would be enough for each of them to have a little bit, Jesus, the miracle Worker, insisted they should bring the obtainable food. All Gospel writers testify that Jesus blessed and served that inadequate food to all present there; plus as John states, besides everyone had their fill as much as they wanted, the disciples 'filled twelve wicker baskets with fragments from the five barley loaves that had been more than they could eat.

Referring to this awesome miracle of Jesus the preachers underline that our Lord does not ask us to meet every need we come across in others' lives. We are only asked to do what we can and leave the rest to him as he works out his loving plan for each human soul. Our supply may be very meager as the disciples brought; but when it was offered in faith to Jesus, it was found to be enough to feed multitudes. And so will be our apparently skimpy efforts of mercy-filled acts. When we dedicate them-not only our efforts of mercy but also the bulk of needs and demands we observe among the poor, the needy, the afflicted and the dying, in truth and in Spirit to our Master in prayer, he can work miracles with such little offerings.

Some critics against the dimension of interceding in Christian prayer quote Jesus's advice on how our prayer should be: "When you are praying, do not heap up empty phrases as the Gentiles do; for they think that they will be heard because of their many words. Do not be like them, for your Father knows what you need before you ask him (Matt. 6:7–8). They are right Jesus does not want a long prayer of interceding for our personal needs. This advice on prayer came to augment his recommendation of 'anawim' spirit his disciples should possess. He wanted us to depend on our Father totally for our needs of existence but expected us to hang on to the filial trust to God who knows what you need before you ask him.

However through Paul Jesus's Spirit reveals to us the importance of intercessory prayer which Paul performed as his habitual act of mercy. If we see through all his prayers for others in his Letters, we discover the central theme of his intercessions has been for their total salvation. Praying for his Jewish brethren he states: My heart's desire and prayer to God on their behalf is for salvation (Rom. 10:1); he thanked God for the salvation bestowed to the Gentiles and interceded to him for strengthening the salvific faith of his converted Christians. For this reason I kneel before the Father, from whom every family in heaven and on earth is named, that he may grant you in accord with the riches of his glory to be strengthened with power through his Spirit in the inner self, and that Christ may dwell in your hearts through faith; that you, rooted and grounded in love, may have strength to comprehend with all the holy ones what is the breadth and length and height and depth, and to know the love of Christ that surpasses knowledge, so that you may be filled with all the fullness of God (Eph. 3:14–19; ref. also Col. 3:9–11; 2 Thess. 1:11–12).

Paul never missed in any one of his intercessions to thank the Lord's marvelous CHESED deeds for his Christian brethren. He emphasizes it in all his Letters: I do not cease giving thanks for you, remembering you in my prayers (Eph. 1:16; ref. also Phil. 1:3-4; 1 Thess. 1:2-4; Phil. 1:4-6). His intercessory prayer was day and night, constant, regular and unceasing. I am grateful to God, whom I worship with a clear conscience as my ancestors did, as I remember you constantly in my prayers, night and day (2 Tim. 1: 3; ref. also Col. 1:9-14; 1 Thess. 1:2-4; 1 Thess. 3:9-13).

Following the footsteps of Paul our Church from its dawn till this day never ceases to encourage all her members the importance and the duty of intercessory prayers for the living, especially for those who are in dire need of liberation, peace, joy, strength and fulfillment. We are instructed by the Church Catechism that our prayer should include petition and intercession along with adoration, praise and thanksgiving etc. The element of petition stresses our feelings of yearning, groaning and pleading as an anawim presenting our poverty and of the entire humanity. (Art. 2629-33). According to the same Catholic Catechism the dimension of 'intercession' in Christian prayer is a prayer of petition which leads us to pray as Jesus did. He is the one intercessor with the Father on behalf of all men, especially sinners. He is able for all time to save those who draw near to God through him, since he always lives to make intercession for them. The Holy Spirit himself intercedes for us and intercedes for the saints according to the will of God (Art. 2634).

From beginning days of the Church we observe the potent force of intercessory prayer. Thanks to God's merciful act of making us partakers in Jesus's victory over sin and death, we have the authority as sons and daughters of God to pray for others, pushing back the darkness of sin and oppression. God invites us to use this powerful weaponry of prayer, as all the Apostles and Saints did, as we seek not only personal transformation but the transformation of the world as well.

The ammunition of Christian intercessory prayer has been bestowed by Christ and above all, it gets its excellent 'signature' of efficacy from the fact of faith that not only Christ's Spirit intercedes with us being present inside our hearts, but also Christ, with his eternal priesthood, stands in front of the throne of God offering his own intercessions for the humanity along with ours. He (Christ), because he remains forever, has a priesthood that does not pass away. Therefore, he is always able to save those who approach God through him, since he lives forever to make intercession for them (Heb. 7:24-25).

Generally our intercessory prayer for others should contain petitions: for God's mercy in forgiveness of their sins; for their healing and deliverance; for their protection from the evil one; for their sanctification; for their unity in diversity; for their safety and security; for establishment and victory of God's justice in and around them; and surely for their spiritual enlightenment. While all these petitions are recommended by Jesus and his Apostles, I feel, praying for justice as Psalmist pleads for, is little hard to digest. However it is very clear if we deeply analyze the CHESED character and his deeds as we did in previous chapters we can appreciate this petition very well. The unjust system prevailing in the human society and among many individuals of arrogance, ignorance and spiritual blindness, has been messing with the right order Jesus's intended to establish as God's Kingdom and doing havoc to the entire human society which is more than ever before crowded with the poorer, the needier and the lowlier humans. Permitting such ongoing injustice within the globe would be one of the practices most likely to bring God's wrath. We know our God is a God of justice. When our Master taught us his Prayer, keeping this fact in his mind, he included the petition 'Thy Kingdom come'. In any situation where we know that injustice is being done, especially in the case of the unjust and cruel persecution of the citizens socially and religiously, we should pray for justice to be done, tempered, of course, by God's mercy.

Finally regarding the efficacy of the merciful disciples' prayer for others we must not forget the benevolence of our Master sharing with us his power of healing the sick by our prayers. Gospel writers remembered to include the Lord's CHESED deeds of healing while he was in this world and they added also his assignment or call for his disciples to perform the same. Since he knew their limitations he promised to share his powerful Spirit of healing. In few places in the Gospels we too read Jesus's disciples did perform such healings by laying hands on them, and by anointing them with oil. More these healing gesture and matter, Jesus indicated to them it must be blended with the prayer of faith (Matt. 17:14–21) and fasting (Mark 9:28–29).

James the Apostle esteeming Jesus's exhortation very seriously he advises us to heal the sick and suffering with our "prayer of faith." Instructing us to pray in strong faith, not doubting, and not with two minds (James 1:6–8), he also recommends to the sick, besides their personal prayer, get the help of the community elders. Is anyone among you sick? He should summon the presbyters of the church, and they should pray over him and anoint [him] with oil in the name of the Lord, and the prayer of faith will save the sick person, and the Lord will raise him up. If he has committed any sins, he will be forgiven. (Jas. 5: 14-15) He insists the need of intercessory prayer for one another. . . . pray for one another, that you may be healed. The fervent prayer of a righteous person is very powerful (James 5:16)

Special Word on Praying for the Dead

While some of our Christian friends don't accept the need of praying for the dead, due to so many overwhelming witness of the early Christian monuments in favor of this kind of prayer, no historian any longer denies that the practice and the belief of it were universally upheld in the primitive Church. Also it is well proven by historians that the practice of praying for the dead existed in Judaism which Christianity inherited from Orthodox Judaism and continued up to this day with no break of continuity in both religions. (Ref. The Catholic Encyclopedia) Except the Lutheran Church and some other churches, the mainline churches preserve this mercy-oriented practice of praying for the dead.

This spiritual act of mercy comes out of many elements of our Christian faith. First our biblically revealed truths about human death. What exactly is death? It depends on whom we ask. To the ordinary person, death is when a human stops breathing. To a doctor, it is when human brain waves stop. Those are reasonable ways of deciding the point of death. But there is more to us than a physical body. From the Christian perspective, what happens to us at death is far less important than what we do at death. The Spirit of Jesus has informed us that death is that point when we sum up our whole life, when a whole lifetime of actions has determined who we are, when a succession of decisions has defined our personality, when we decide what we want to be for eternity. Death is the instant when we finally acknowledge precisely who we are and then present that finished self as an offering to the mercy of God.

In the true reality of our glorious life, namely death is not an end at all as the Book of Wisdom states: "They seemed, in the view of the foolish, to be dead; and their passing away was thought an affliction and their going forth from us, utter destruction. But they are in peace" (Wis. 3:1-3). Another dimension of that faith is as Paul writes in his Letters, that there is resurrection that preserves the continuity of our life: "We know that if our earthly dwelling, a tent, should be destroyed, we have a building from God, a dwelling not made with hands, eternal in heaven" (2 Cor. 5:1). Our Christian faith about our life after death is also based on the assurance Jesus our Master gave to us: "Everything that the Father gives me will come to me, and I will not reject anyone who comes to me . . . This is the will of the one who sent me that I should not lose anything of what he gave me, but that I should raise it on the last day" (John 6: 37-39).

In this modern world many may not agree or adhere to our Christian faith in eternal after death because they seem to be farfetched wild dreams. However we say they realities and human certainties. A brilliant English physicist and chemist, scientist, Sir Michael Faraday, who lived in 18th century, has contributed a lot to the understanding of electro magnetism. While he was on his death bed some journalists asked him about his speculations about life after death. He replied: "Speculations! I know nothing about speculations. I am resting on certainties." That is what every Christian live and move and survive with peacefully in this valley of tears.

Within this astounding faith-parameter we are exhorted that even though separated from our earthly body in death, we yet continue a personal existence; and that during this stage, by God's CHESED those who've died in a state of grace are already taken to a blissful realm, named Heaven; but those who unfortunately die without sanctifying grace are thrown into the eternal suffering place, named hell. Besides there may be others among the dead who've died seemingly without repentance but still possess interiorly the warmth of grace and not having sins against the 'Holy Spirit'. Therefore, I say to you, every sin and blasphemy will be forgiven people, but blasphemy against the Spirit will not be forgiven. And whoever speaks a word against the Son of Man will be forgiven; but whoever speaks against the Holy Spirit will not be forgiven, either in this age or in the age to come (Matt. 12:31-32).

Expounding this extraordinary 'speculation' the Church teaches us that there is an intrinsic connection between the living and the dead as 'communion of saints'. We the living are members of the 'pilgrim Church'; among the dead those who rest in eternal peace and bliss already before the face of God are members of the 'heavenly Church'; and there is also the 'suffering Church' in this world which is made of those pilgrims passing through patiently, enduring the trials and persecutions and sufferings for the sake of their purification and salvation. In addition to this living group of sufferers for their sins,

Church invites us to believe the same kind of 'suffering Church' (purgatory) existing in the other world where many of our deceased brethren live. These are the ones who have not yet entered the heavenly bliss, waiting and longing for the bountiful mercy of God to be purified from all their impurity and unholiness that obstruct their entrance to the Mansions of Holy of Holies. It is for these sufferers 'the merciful' are asked to intercede to the Lord of mercy to look upon them with merciful eyes and grant eternal rest.

Though we may theologically and Biblically divide the dead into three groups of living after death in accordance with the God's justice, feeble humans as we are, we may not fathom out fully with Paul, the depth of the riches and wisdom and knowledge of God; his inscrutable judgements and his unsearchable ways of mercy. (Ref. Rom. 11: 30-35) Therefore we don't know exactly the status of the dead and so we are instructed to pray generally for all the faithful departed. The prayers we, the merciful' lisp for them, according to our traditional belief, will add to their own pleading to get the mercy of God. Though redemption has been once for all brought by Jesus, still we believe God's eternal mercy demands our intercessions added to Jesus's eternal prayer in heaven. Those of us who are enlightened by the above-stated Biblical and historical points on Christian faith related to the interactions existing between the eternal mercy of holiest God and eternal destiny of purified unholy humans continue to pray daily remembering our beloved dead: Eternal rest grant unto him/her (them), O Lord; and let perpetual light shine upon him/her (them). May he/she (they) rest in peace. And may the souls of the faithful departed, through the mercy of God, rest in peace. Amen.

This is how our act of praying for the dead gets its qualification of the "act of mercy," through which being merciful to our suffering brothers and sisters we authenticate and proclaim the unfathomable sovereignty of God's mercy and justice.

CHAPTER 22

Chesed Action 6

Unassumingly Doing Corporal Works of Mercy

An exhortation of Saint Theresa of Avila spells out the valid reasons for our untiring corporal works of mercy: "Christ has no body on earth now but yours, no hands but yours, no feet but yours. Yours are the eyes through which the compassion of Christ must look out on the world. Yours are the feet with which He is to go about doing good. Yours are the hands with which He is to bless His people." St. Theresa rightly echoes what the King Jesus shared with us about his final judgment over the humans (Matt. 25:31-46): "And the king will say to them in reply, Amen, I say to you, whatever you did for one of these least brothers of mine, you did for me . . . He will answer them, Amen, I say to you, what you did not do for one of these least ones, you did not do for me."

Too often, works of mercy become a humanistic endeavor where one feels obligated to help out of peer pressure or because it's the thing to do, and one will gain some temporal reward either financially or in praise and so they become philanthropic without realizing it. Too many fail to realize that for something to truly be a work of mercy and gain merit in heaven, it must be done out of love for our neighbor because of our love for God first and foremost. Without God as the keystone of all we do, all is futile. That is why the corporal works of mercy cannot stand on their own without the spiritual works of mercy. Yet both are vital in our cooperation with salvation for ourselves and our neighbors.

The Spirit of God insists consistently that the Creator's sole preoccupation is implementation of his CHESED and chivalrous acts as the champion of the poor, the oppressed, and the needy. Blessed be the one whose help is the God of Jacob; whose hope is in the LORD, his God, the Maker of heaven and earth, the seas, and all that is in them; who keeps faith forever, secures justice for the oppressed; who gives bread to the hungry. The LORD sets prisoners free; the LORD gives sight to the blind. The LORD raises up those who are bowed down; the LORD loves the righteous. The LORD protects the resident alien, comes to the aid of the orphan and the widow, but thwarts the way of the wicked. The LORD shall reign forever, your God, Zion, through all generations! (Ps. 146:2–10).

God's faithful children like Tobit, meticulously and conscientiously fulfilled our God's covenantal demand from them to imitate his CHESED. They too advised their children, saying,

> Give alms from your possessions. Do not turn your face away from any of the poor, so that God's face will not be turned away from you. Give in proportion to what you own. If you have great wealth, give alms out

> of your abundance; if you have but little, do not be afraid to give alms even of that little. You will be storing up a goodly treasure for yourself against the day of adversity. For almsgiving delivers from death and keeps one from entering into Darkness. Almsgiving is a worthy offering in the sight of the Most High for all who practice it. (Tobit 4:7–11)

Jesus confirms this propelling manifesto of his Father, and in that spirit, he started his CHESED undertakings both in word and deed about which Peter testified to the gathering at the house of Cornelius:

> God anointed Jesus of Nazareth with the Holy Spirit and power. He went about doing good and healing all those oppressed by the devil, for God was with him. We are witnesses of all that he did both in the country of the Jews and (in) Jerusalem. (Acts 10:38–39)

Jesus too, sending his Spirit to his disciples and anointing them by the Power from on high, willed and commissioned them to go throughout the world to perform his CHESED role both in word and deed (Luke and Matthew).

Our Master and King Christ, in his narration of the "final judgment," lists out the corporal acts of mercy any merciful should perform if they desire to get crowned as "the blessed."

Corporal Act of Mercy 1

Telling "I was hungry and you gave me food," Jesus expects us to reach out to the hungry whoever and wherever they are. Our heart must be one like Jesus's compassionate heart, which was throbbing at the sight of the hungry.

> My heart is moved with pity for the crowd, for they have been with me now for three days and have nothing to eat. I do not want to send them away hungry, for fear they may collapse on the way. (Matt. 15:32)

Merciful acts toward the hungry does not stop by merely providing one meal or two. As the modern axiom indicates, "It is better to teach how to fish than to provide fish." It means that those who are energetic and capable of working, if they are unemployed, may become incapable of feeding themselves and their families. The merciful should work together in preventing unemployment. They will help out best by giving work to all they can afford to help; work is better for the able-bodied than direct almsgiving. The act of feeding the hungry includes also making donations to the local food bank and helping at a local soup kitchen for the homeless. If possible, we must educate ourselves and our family members about the problem of hunger in the world, and we can use our political voices to inspire our community members to fight against world hunger and make it a higher priority.

The Food and Agriculture Organization (FAO) is a specialized agency of the United Nations that leads international efforts to defeat hunger. It is present in 130 countries in the world, and its world headquarters is in Rome. Its Latin motto *Fiat panis* translates into English as "Let there be bread." Obviously, the world organization has the noble intention of finding out ways and means of eliminating the problem of hunger in the world. According to its recent study, worldwide, every single day, almost 16,000 children die from hunger-related causes. In the United States, according to Bread for the World, a Christian group urging our nation's leaders to end hunger at home and abroad, one out of every four children is "at risk of hunger" and more than one out of every five children live in households that "struggle to put food on the table."

We, the disciples of Jesus, feel proud of the fact that the origin of many globally coordinated community efforts is nothing but the compassionate heart of Jesus Christ. In his godly heart, he foresaw the personal and social difficulties of the whole human race, and he put forward to us a way, a weird but genuine ritual, but resourceful and personal but combined with communal dimension. That is the tradition of celebrating the Eucharist. Through the historical ritual of breaking of Christ's Body and shedding of his Blood, Jesus established a very resourceful way to feed the hungry in all possible ways.

Connecting the Eucharistic ritual and "merciful actual," Blessed Mother Teresa of Calcutta was quoted as avowing that there are two kinds of "Real Presence" of our Lord in this world: the Lord's Real Presence in the Blessed Sacrament, where he fills us with his light, his life, and his love, and our Lord's real presence in the poor, both in those materially poor and those spiritually poor, where he is waiting for us to give him back his light, his life, and his love. Living on the Bread of Life, we receive our Savior's merciful love, sharing our bread with those who hunger physically and spiritually, we return that love back to Him, giving His compassionate Heart solace and joy.

Though the Eucharist is a mystery, it has made history of its own—the history of feeding daily millions of hungry people around the world. This is why the famous Hindu saint Mohandas Gandhi is quoted as saying once: "If Christ ever comes to India, he'd better come as bread."

Corporal Act of Mercy 2

Jesus promised those who give a cup of cold water will not go unrewarded (Mark 9:40). NT writers prove that Jesus, being born human as we are, experienced thirst, especially while at dying on the cross. It was a clear sign of excruciating suffering. We read in the Gospels about Jesus's thirst. According to them, he was crucified at 9:00 a.m. (Mark 15:25); that is, between 9:00 a.m. and 12:00 noon and he was hanging on the cross till 3:00 p.m. (Mark 15:33).

During this noon hours of horrible scorching sun, naturally, any Palestinian Jew would have felt thirsty, and Jesus, being tormented by horrible suffering and pain and emptied of his entire blood and water, would have certainly felt unbearable thirst. We hear Gospel writers telling us that his enemies, as a mockery and with hatred, gave him only a sort of wine, mostly a type of vinegar; he couldn't taste it. And such horrific thirst might have been one of the causes for his death. As John put it, going through such agony of thirst as the final climactic CHESED action of mercy, Jesus died, saying, "It is finished" (John 19:28–30).

Water is one of the most essential sources for life on earth. Therefore, water, to put it bluntly, is a matter of life and death. By life experience, we know humans can survive quite a long time without food, but we will die within days if we don't get water. In many respects, giving drink to the thirsty is also giving them life. In particular, this demand of Jesus places before our eyes millions of God's children who don't have enough and healthy and pure drinking water, who perennially look up to the sky for the rain to cultivate their lands and supply water to their cattle. We join our generous hands together as one global family in supporting the projects of constructing reservoirs and purifying public drinking water, etc., as best as we can.

To so many people in the world, particularly in developing countries, a clean and reliable supply of fresh water is only a dream. An estimated 884 million lack access to a supply of safe water. Over 3.5 million people a year die from water-related diseases. Every twenty seconds, a child in the world dies of such diseases. Nearly one-fifth of all childhood deaths are caused by diarrhea, which kills more young children than AIDS, TB, and malaria combined (ref. www.water.org).

Giving water to the thirsty may begin with a cup or bottle, but it is a more lasting gift if it means helping them to dig a well, create a simple pit toilet, or stopping people from polluting our lakes, streams, rivers, and groundwater supplies. Many of us who live near the Great Lakes or other large sources of fresh water can easily take it for granted. We can drink, shower, sprinkle our lawns, wash our cars, and flush our toilets without really thinking about it.

I read in the same blog, in water.org, that an American taking a five-minute shower uses more water than a typical person in a developing country slum uses in a whole day. Conserving water, especially in our own homes, refraining from polluting waterways or streams, protecting local watersheds, and supporting conservation efforts that benefit streams, rivers, and sources of groundwater are some ways of enacting the work of mercy.

In addition, we can do small but very extraordinary acts of mercy, such as giving someone a drink on a hot day, giving the baby its bottle, pouring drinks at the table, and lifting up a young child to get a drink at a water fountain, and so on.

Corporal Act of Mercy 3

We are ordered by the King Jesus to clothe the naked as if clothing him as the King's proxy. It is a continuous affirmation in scriptures that if a person is just in front of God, he would perform, besides faith-oriented rituals, the acts of mercy such as clothing the naked (Ref. Ezra 18:5–7). Job, talking to his friends about his fear of God with which he had been living from his childhood, added that he had never missed clothing the naked wanderers and poor people (ref. Job 31:19–20). When people were jolted by John the Baptizer's statement about the final end of those who didn't bear good fruits in life, they asked him in anxiety, "What then should we do?" He replied, "Whoever has two tunics should share with the person who has none" (Luke 3:9–11).

To be naked means to be in a state of having had one's clothes stripped off. This act of stripping can be either by oneself as we read in OT about Noah's nakedness (Gen. 9:20–23) or by others like Jesus who was stripped naked by the agents of Satan while he was hanging on the cross. It is a universal understanding among the humans that clothes preserve the human dignity. We are aware of the despicable condition of millions of humans around the globe staying nearly naked with no proper clothes to shield them from cold or heat and shame. Clothing them means we do what God did to our first parents, dressing them with garments of skin (Gen. 3:21) and what Christ elevated to a high gesture of love to him, namely, we would be clothing the Son of the Living God, who will not forget it on our final Judgment Day.

Undeniably, to obey the King's order, personally clothing the naked, is the best act. However, as what our church tradition upholds throughout the centuries, we can clean out closets and donate the extras to the charitable agencies like Catholic Charities, Vincent de Paul Society, and Salvation Army who would hand out on our behalf those clothes to the needy. To go a little more in this regard, we should simplify our lives and cut buying costly, exuberant clothes; and instead of donating the used and outgrown clothes, we should buy new basic clothes to those in really need of such ones. This means it's not just about giving unwanted things away but about owning less and offering support to those who don't have enough.

I fully agree with what Mark Shea wrote in *National Catholic Register* (May 31, 2014), summing up this universal Catholic merciful act of clothing the naked:

> As a general rule, the command to clothe the naked is concerned primarily not with the need for human warmth, but with the need

for human dignity . . . Our task as Catholics is to clothe the naked in accord with that grammar and to acknowledge their human dignity thereby. It is to remember that clothes were made for man, not man for clothes—and that, above all, we are to put off the old nature and put on the new nature, which is being renewed in knowledge after the image of its Creator.

Corporal Act of Mercy 4

Remembering the CHESED act of our God in Jesus in setting the prisoners free, we should visit the imprisoned. Many suspect that such an act of mercy may seem like being soft on crime. Men of goodwill never hesitate to follow a balanced and enlightened principle that any punishment to the sinners should prevent, confine, and give the accused the opportunity to do penance and come back once again to live a second chance, a life of purity. Our Christian act of mercy of visiting these prisoners, combined with friendship and prayer is capable of bringing out such reformation and healing to the prisoners.

Hence, the merciful visit prisoners, not necessarily to work for their freeing, which surely can be done if possible, but with more concern and understanding toward them. We should pay visits to them, console them, give material help, and above all, instruct them to forgive their enemies if they are unjustly put in jail and to melt their hearts to turn to the Supreme Master for his forgiveness if they truly deserve the punishment and try to rehabilitate them in renewed life. Unquestionably by the justice of God and for the safety of the human family, society has little choice but lock the violent criminals up (if they are rightly judged) and throw away the key. As one spiritual author writes, "Throw away the key, indeed but not the person."

Besides visiting prisoners, we can perform some more solid acts of mercy for the imprisoned, such as fighting for humane treatment for the imprisoned, helping to care for the families of the imprisoned, protecting children from adult abusers.

Corporal Act of Mercy 5

To shelter the homeless is literally the true act of a Good Samaritan. There are thousands and thousands of our brethren in the world, who may be in our own neighborhood who don't have any place to lie down and no roof to shelter in the heavy winter and scorching summer. They are reminding us of Jesus of Nazareth who pointed out his miserable vagabond-styled life: "Foxes have dens and birds of the sky have nests, but the Son of Man has nowhere to rest his head" (Matt. 8:20).

It is to these poor we are compelled by our Master to provide clean and comfortable homes, free of charge or at low rates of rent. Under this category of merciful act of offering shelter, we should include one of the most humane and even divine acts of giving hospitality to strangers and pilgrims. This is what Jesus meant when he said, "A stranger and you welcomed me." The letter to the Hebrews very well wrote, "Do not neglect hospitality, for through it some have unknowingly entertained angels" (Heb. 13:2).

Homelessness is a very real and often unseen form of suffering in our community. Those who live in slum areas of many countries, millions of people, live in cardboard, straw, and thatched homes; some people live in homes made of discarded materials; many people are literally homeless living and sleeping in street corners and public places.

As we see in many parishes around the world, each winter, parishioners can be invited to volunteer at the local homeless shelters or collect some fund to be donated for such shelters in other parts of the world. For example, wherever I have been serving, I invited my parishioners to do the same every year and sent the collected fund to three homes of mercy in India, sponsored by an Oklahoman charitable agency, Green Cross Ministries Inc., where abused children, HIV/AIDS affected and infected children, and neglected seniors are offered safe and healthy shelter, food, and clothes. Volunteering for Habitat for Humanity or other organizations that provide affordable housing is another means of fulfilling this work of mercy.

Let us also do something like bringing others to our homes in times of fire, floods, or other disasters, helping the seniors and disabled people to take care of their house, dusting the furniture, making the beds, cleaning the floor, and cutting the grass.

Corporal Act of Mercy 6

The act of visiting the sick has already been discussed, focusing the core of that act as a spiritual healing. Because of this act of caring for the sick, in blessing us, Jesus will tell us, "I was ill and you cared for me." Here, as a corporal act, Jesus insists on our bodily and emotional presence at the side of the sick. Usually the community calls these people who visit the sick as caregivers.

I am sure like me, all of us feel isolated and lonely more at the time of being hospitalized or bedridden because of illness. Human hearts crave for the loving visits of their relatives and friends. At this juncture of human life, we need to pay a visit to them as loving brothers and sisters in the Lord or as doctors, nurses, and as counselors. The same act of mercy can be enlarged, if our financial condition permits, by building, supporting, or aiding a hospital or a patronage for the sick. This "caregiving ministry" is the most meritorious act of mercy.

Qualified doctors and nurses donate their services to provide free medical care for those who cannot afford any. There are inner-city parishes in the United States that have done much the same thing. In part then, to "comfort the sick" means, first of all, to comfort them with something they urgently need: namely, proper medical assistance. Sadly, in the United States today, approximately 40 million people have to rely almost exclusively on the hospital emergency rooms for family or personal medical care because they cannot afford to purchase medical insurance. An adequate medical safety net for the poor is still badly needed.

Of course, there are some people who are "sick" not from physical illness but from social isolation. One thinks especially of the elderly in our communities who, whether at home or in long-term care facilities, live in geographical isolation from their loved ones. "Visiting the sick" in our world can mean reaching out to the friendless in our local nursing homes: those who are "sick at heart" from being lonely and forgotten and who are regularly deprived of the basic human need called "friendship." The socially isolated elderly are usually not far away. They often live just around the corner from us or are members of our own parish. Simply volunteer with the Meals-on-Wheels program and you will find them. Most of all, we should not forget that some of them may even be members of our own family, relatives too much overlooked and too often forgotten.

I want to share with the readers a personal story on this caregiving ministry to the seniors in our families, which put me on the right track of Christian life. Once, I went to a village to participate in the First Mass celebrated by one of my seminary companions in his native village. In his first homily, he was thanking all his mentors, friends, and beneficiaries. One among them was his dad who was sixty-five years old. The priest in a moving way described how his father helped him to realize the true meaning of mass.

He said, "My dad was a regular daily mass goer. He always made sure I was accompanying him, but I was too sleepy. How could have I been awake that early at five in the morning? However, he took me daily to the mass. What surprised me was my dad would leave soon after communion, leaving me in the church with other boys and girls to attend catechism classes. I was a bit curious about his behavior. So one day, I decided to follow him to find out why he was hurrying. I sneaked out of the church and followed behind him. He went into the home, never to the bathroom as I had thought. Instead he went into the room where my grandma was sleeping. I was watching standing near the door; I was stunned to notice what he was doing as my grandma was ninety-five years old, bedridden, immovable, but breathing, eating, etc. My dad started cleaning up the mess she had done at night to her dresses and bed with the peeing and pooing. He took my grandma to the restroom and cleaned her, put on her new clothes, and kept her in the armchair. He went to her bed, removed all the dirtied clothes, took them to the laundry room. He came again, cleaned the bed, placed a new bedspread, blanket, etc. He moved my grandma to her bed again and told her, 'Mama, I will soon be back with breakfast.' I hid myself, and he went and prepared some hot oatmeal and egg, etc., with hot coffee. He sat near my grandma and fed her gently, warmly, and smilingly. He kissed her and left the room.

"I ran to the entrance of my home, but unfortunately he saw me running, caught hold of me, and asked me, 'What are you doing?' I explained what I did and begged his pardon. He did pardon me; he smiled at me, and both of us went to wake up my sickly mother. After a day when my dad was relaxed, I asked him: "Dad, why do you come out of the church before mass ends? Don't you like to stay back for other prayers and rituals?" He said, "My son, the Mass we attend in the church is only a ritual. What I do at home soon after mass, as you saw, is the actual mass God is more pleased with. If you become a priest, if it fits you, you also must make people understand this." I said okay at that time without understanding much." After narrating this story, the new priest, who was shedding tears, went to his dad who was then seventy-five years; and though he was blind, he was smiling. The priest hugged him and kissed him.

What an amazing story it was that I heard and the inspiring incident I attended. It was unforgettable. This is what Jesus did and exhorts us to do today. Whenever we are dismissed at the end of Mass, while we respond "thanks be to God," we should say to ourselves, "Come on, let us go out soon and visit the sick, the dying, the unfortunate, the homeless, the needy, the poor, and the weak to console, to feed, to strengthen them as best as we can." That is the real and meaningful Mass we should perform every day that will please God more than anything else.

Visiting the housebound elderly and the chronically and terminally ill is no easy task. Trying to do it on a regular basis can take us right out of our "comfort zones" because it confronts us with real human lives for which, in earthly terms, there seems to be so little hope. Such people often live in squalor and with the constant stench of sickness or the wince of chronic pain. But our mere presence, as someone willing to be a friend and a listening ear, can mean much more to them than we can imagine, and along the way, they will be giving a precious gift to us as well: the gift of growth in the virtue of compassion.

Corporal Act of Mercy 7

It is the grateful and dignified act of burying the dead. The ritual act of giving farewell to the dead has been the revealed and humane custom of all humans. It is endorsed and encouraged by all religions, but the mode of it differs from each other according to each one's culture. While some perform the ritual of burning the dead, others do it by burying the dead. All these rituals have been done with respect and sometimes solemnly.

In Christianity, which is an offshoot of Judaism (Rom. 11:16–24), the ritual of burying the dead has been followed in the footsteps of the patriarchs of Judaism. We can read in OT how meticulously and respectfully this ritual had been observed and handed down to the later generation. The *what*, *why*, and *how* of it was very beautifully portrayed by the instruction of the wise teacher Sirach:

> My son, shed tears for one who is dead with wailing and bitter lament; as is only proper, prepare the body, and do not absent yourself from the burial. Weeping bitterly, mourning fully, pay your tribute of sorrow, as deserved. (Sir. 38:16–17)

The best role model in this merciful act was Tobit, an amazing moral and just person shown in the OT. In the book of Tobit, the writer uses the autobiographical style of his time, telling of Tobit's life and virtues and all of his undertakings. We are told, besides many charitable deeds, that Tobit was regularly burying the dead, especially those who died and were never cared for by neighbors and relatives. For performing such a generous action, he was persecuted and was being hunted by his enemies to be put to death; he even lost all his property but never gave up his charity and continued this chivalrous act till his death (Tobit 1:16–20). Tobit too instructed his beloved son Tobiah to continue doing the same merciful deeds as he had done and also added that he and his wife must be buried decently with the same respect he has been burying his neighbors (ref. Tobit 4:3).

The merciful act of burying the dead includes certainly taking special care of planning and executing an appropriate Christian burial to our family members;

many among us before our death, living with a healthy mind, make note of how our burial should be decently and liturgically performed. I have witnessed the prompt and sincere obedience of young ones in fulfilling their parents' wish. As community members, we too have the duty and gratitude of attending the funerals of our neighbors, visiting their houses of mourning, and aiding the bereaved families. The advice of Paul, weep with those who weep (Rom. 12:15), has to be practiced in the time of death of others.

Humans as we are, there are many in our community who are grieving and struggling to bury their dead emotionally. It takes for them a long and arduous process to be healed; shedding tears at a funeral day is insufficient. As a merciful act, we, the disciples of Jesus, must help these grieving friends to truly bury their lost loved ones by letting go of them, entrusting them to the hands of our merciful Creator and Savior. This is what the great wise teacher Sirach instructs us:

> Weeping bitterly, mourning fully, pay your tribute of sorrow, as deserved. A day or two, to prevent gossip; then compose yourself after your grief. For grief can bring on death, and heartache can sap one's strength. When a person is carried away, sorrow is over; and the life of the poor one is grievous to the heart. Do not turn your thoughts to him again; cease to recall him; think rather of the end. Do not recall him, for there is no hope of his return; you do him no good, and you harm yourself. Remember that his fate will also be yours; for him it was yesterday, for you today.

> With the dead at rest, let memory cease;
> be consoled, once the spirit has gone. (Sir.
> 38:17–23)

Mere preaching at the pulpit won't be effective in this matter of consoling the grieving people. It takes friendship and faith-filled fellowship to continue visiting the bereaved and patiently holding friendly conversations in helping them dry their tears.

FINAL NOTE

Elohim shall send forth His **chesed**
and His emes.

—Psalm 57:(3)4, OJB

May <u>God</u> send his faithful love
and his constancy!

— Psalm 57:(3)4, NJB

The Global Blunder of Ignoring the **CHESED** *of God*

There are some things in life we can count on with great confidence, such as the brightness of stars, the inconsistency of man, and much more so regarding the mercy of the loving and forgiving God because of his fidelity, one more of his attributes. The most critical truth that we humans find extremely hard to accept is that "mercy of God" is about our lack of deserving the gift presented. We need to accept mercy from the Supreme because we don't deserve to be treated as innocent. The mind-blowing anomaly in this act of God's mercy is, as Paul writes, "But God, who is rich in mercy, because of the great love he had for us, even when we were dead in our transgressions, brought us to life with Christ by grace you have been saved" (Eph. 2:4-5). This is entirely because of God's innate nature CHESED' and of our own inherent sinfulness.

The God whom we serve was the first to move toward us out of his CHESED, with his eternal merciful hands to embrace us even when we were dead in our sins. Surprisingly, he continues to stand by us with his love when we fail to be faithful to our covenantal promises to Him; indeed we have betrayed, lied about, forgotten, tarnished, and denied his CHESED calling. Nonetheless, he is there very closely walking with us, waiting patiently for our return. We behave like a scorpion, which bit again and again a kindhearted person who rescued it from drowning in water. When asked about his useless and thankless effort, the generous soul retorted, "Scorpion did as its nature is, and I too did my rescuing task according to my nature." Yes, that is what is happening between God and ourselves: whether we do his will or not, God acts as a merciful Father because of his faithful nature.

I discovered in my personal life that if only we can let the mercy of God in its original and genuine meaning be the foundation of our lives, our entire dissipated and distorted dark cloudy life will be renewed and reassembled with joy and fullness. We will feel fully secure and be settled in the unshakable Ark of the Covenant though we may from time to time ride on fast-running horses of earthly hunting; this is because we made sure we are saddled not simply on horses but on the CHESED of the Almighty. Then we won't need some artificial man-made safety networks such as race, color, caste, creed, or politics as our comfort zone. Psychologically, we will be freed of fear, hate, guilt, or pusillanimity and begin to be open to our any sort of neighbors despite their social or personal profiles.

The greatest "mercy effect" is we will extend our forgiveness and mercy toward even our enemies. Our Christian attitude will be developed slowly but steadily into the likeness of God's tender mercy, inexhaustible compassion, and unconditional love. One thing I can testify. All the mercy-filled actions that I perform or practice my faith commands me to do are not to condition God's mercy or justice in any way. That is plainly a blasphemy against the Sovereignty of God; it also may be a kind of childish way of viewing human life. Rather, all that I am religiously engaged in are truthfully my human CHESED response to the first love-move of my Primary Partner in covenantal deal. Any accomplishment I undertake in the spiritual or religious realms is only to demonstrate my inner drive of offering my thanks, appreciation, plus my steadfastness to fulfill the CHESED. I may fail or flung; it doesn't matter to the merciful God whom I know is eternally magnanimous and loving. He smiles at me a spoiled brat, but like a benevolent parent, stays with me till my last breath. "Because his mercy endures forever!"

As we are journeying in the Year of Mercy, the pope and his messengers send us to many directions for how to confront the daunting challenges of mercy in this postmodern culture. Pope Francis, talking about this beautiful but dangerous culture, said in his remarks at the World Meeting of Families 2015:

> Today's culture seems to encourage people not to bond with anything or anyone, not to trust. Competition and consumption are the guiding principles, a consumption which does not favor bonding, a consumption which has little to do

with human relationships. The result is a "radical loneliness" and fear of commitment.

One of the pope's messengers, Cardinal Pietro Parolin, in his interview with French Catholic newspaper *La Croix* (November 16, 2015), confirmed the papal remark by saying,

It is time for an "offensive of mercy" since the world is so torn by violence. Besides listing out some means to deal with this bizarre culture, the cardinal observed: A mobilization which would involve all spiritual resources to provide a positive response to evil.

Let's Do Merciful Acts as Many as We Can or At Least Pray

Of course you can't, and no one is asking you to do so. Not all these things. Perhaps just two or three, as you have the opportunity. To accept the challenge of being a true disciple of Jesus Christ, however, means making yourself available to whatever our Lord might call you to do in His service. It means opening your eyes, opening your hearts, and serving His children. It's our duty. Even for those who, through circumstances beyond their control, cannot do much more than they are doing now, they can always pray for those who are doing works of mercy. (Robert Stackpole, STD is director of the John Paul II Institute of Divine Mercy.)

Dr. Stackpole too listed out that those who are unable to do any merciful acts can pray for those who are strenuously performing charity ministries around the globe. Let us remember St. Teresa of Lisieux, who was canonized and made as the doctor of the church, who didn't even go out of her monastery; but it is said that by her continuous prayer, so many souls were converted and had gone to heaven. Prayer of the CHESED-based heartbeats is very powerful.

Let's Do the Merciful Deeds Today, Not Waiting for Tomorrow

In his fine commentary on Matthew's Gospel, William Barclay cited a fable about three apprentice demons who were being sent to earth to complete their apprenticeships. Before they departed, Satan asked each of them how they were going to tempt and ruin humankind. "I will tell them there is no God," said the first. Satan responded, "That will not delude many, for they know there is a God." At that, the second demon said, "I will tell them there is no hell." To that, Satan said, "You will deceive no one, for they also know that there is a hell for the unrepentant." The third demon said, "I will tell them that there is no hurry." Pleased at this response, Satan said, "Go! You will ruin them by the thousands" (*The Daily Study Bible* [United Kingdom: The Saint Andrew Press, Edinburgh, 1975]).

Barclay is correct in expounding the evil of procrastination in Christian life, especially in performing the merciful deeds for which Jesus has called us. The more we procrastinate in doing good deeds, the greater would be Satan's victory over us. We are reminded of this fact in

259

two places of Scriptures. In Proverb 18:9, we read, "*Those slack in their work are kin to the destroyer.*" Also, James writes, "*One who knows the right thing to do and does not do it, it is a sin*" (James 4:17). There may be many reasons sages and psychologists would have listed. I personally take three of them from the online blog *Daily Hope with Rick Warren*:

1. Indecision: Many among us, as James refers (1:6–8) are people of two minds, unstable in all our ways. Sometimes we live like a wave of the sea that is driven and tossed about by the wind. Being undecided with no strong willpower, slothfully we hate this day and wait for tomorrow. The most dangerous of all delusions is to think that there is plenty of time. As one netizen posted, we should do what we have to do today because we don't owe tomorrow, therefore to say "I will do it tomorrow is to infringe in God's territory."

2. Perfectionism: The inspired word hits us, saying, "*One who pays heed to the wind will never sow, and one who watches the clouds will never reap* (Eccles. 11:4). The Living Bible relevantly translates this verse: "*If you wait for perfect conditions, you'll never get anything done!*" That is the unpredictable and imperfect condition of creaturely life. However, we must do the best we can within the available hours.

3. Fear: The scriptural wise saying (Prov. 29:25) is "*Fear of others becomes a snare.*" Due to our human survival tendency of being cautious, most of us are enslaved by the feeling of fear. We are afraid of facing the end results of being good and doing good, such as the rejection and criticism of our neighbors due to their jealousy and misunderstanding. We should clearly know that no one born in this world, including our Master Jesus, have accomplished any great "CHESED deeds" without being

burned or hurt by evil agents. Let us remember this: *No pain, no gain.*

Suffering Also a Significant "Merciful Deed"

In my book *My Religion*, I have extensively discussed about Christian suffering. I have explained that every servant of God is a suffering servant like our Master Jesus who has learned and grown himself through his sufferings as a compassionate and understanding person. He demanded that all those who want to follow him in his "servant life" must drink the same bitterest cup and be bathed by the same bleeding baptism. He and his disciples, like any other humans, have to undergo suffering, pain, sickness, and death as inevitable consequences of human life. But the uniqueness in the God servants' sufferings is that all of their natural sufferings, if borne as Jesus, can be made into some effective instruments of salvation for those whom they are serving.

Suffering is possible only in those beings that move. A stone or a dead body is incapable of feeling the pain and suffering. So suffering enters into our system when we get up and move to do something, even to move the organs of our body, and surely to move from the womb of our mother to the outside world. It is a move from a higher level to lower level. It is a move to serve the other and become even a slave of love and compassion to the other. This is what Jesus meant when he said, *"For the Son of Man did not come to be served but to serve and to give his life as a ransom for many."* He stresses that whenever his disciples suffer for the sake of moving out of themselves as servants to stretch out their merciful hands toward the poor and the needy, that suffering is the greatest resource from heaven. "*You know that those who are recognized as rulers over the Gentiles lord it over them, and their great ones make their authority over them felt. But it shall not be so among you. Rather, whoever wishes to be great among you will be your servant; whoever wishes to be first among you will be the slave of all.*" This is why I want to highlight here that our sufferings can be another form of "merciful acts" to name us "the blessed."

Paul, with full grasp of the mystery of suffering in his apostolate, writes about the glorious benefits of Christian sufferings (2 Cor. 4:7-18). Besides confirming that through our sufferings our entire life would become the manifestation of Jesus's life ("*For we who live are constantly being given up to death for the sake of Jesus, so that the life of Jesus may be manifested in our mortal flesh*") and that we too would earn eternal life after death ("*For this momentary light affliction is producing for us an eternal weight of glory beyond all comparison*"), he inspires us with a statement about another redemptive benefit of sufferings in our CHESED accomplishment. He says that our suffering with Christ will be benefitting to our brothers and sisters in their salvation: "*Everything indeed is for you, so that the grace bestowed in abundance on more and more people may cause the thanksgiving to overflow for the glory of God.*"

Luke quotes Jesus, saying to all who had gathered around him, "*If anyone wishes to come after me, he must deny himself and take up his cross daily and follow me*" (Luke 9:23). Yes, Jesus wanted us to accept the exterior public suffering that results from Christian CHESED involvement in the social, political, and economic issues of society; he meant the hostility, criticism, ridicule, opposition, and condemnation that would come to the merciful who publicly try—by word or action—to right any social wrong in the light of Gospel principles. As I pointed out earlier, even in our merciful acts toward the poor and the needy, we would be facing such sufferings. Jesus pointed out that Christianity is not a quiet haven of private solace and security, but a challenging call to the public suffering of self-sacrificing action.

Certainly, Jesus didn't want us to accomplish all our CHESED-oriented actions as mere humanitarian or philanthropic deeds. Those actions are not bad, but in the Kingdom of God, they won't bear the right and valid fruits. Hence, Jesus added to his demand of taking up our crosses: *"For whoever wishes to save his life will lose it, but whoever loses his life for my sake will save it"* (Luke 9:24). He demands that all the merciful acts we do must be in his name and for his sake—for his values, in his Spirit and in Truth. Many times, fulfilling Jesus's command of love and mercy is hard and involves suffering. Being a helper in the building of the kingdom requires work; plus, it is a real challenge performing the merciful actions in the footsteps and teachings of Jesus—doing the right thing and loving our neighbor can be downright dangerous. But those of us who want to be crowned as "the blessed" must endure as our Master has endured.

> *For the sake of the joy that lay before Jesus he endured the cross, despising its shame, and has taken his seat at the right of the throne of God. Consider how he endured such opposition from sinners, in order that you may not grow weary and lose heart.* (Heb. 12:2-3)

As we read and reflect on Jesus's life and saying, especially about the "cross," we can observe how he in a very positive way accepted the sufferings, embraced them with his full freedom, but always used them for the greater good of the world. He made his own crosses as the wooden platform to gather people together, as the wooden ladder to take them up to greater vision and mission and as the wooden weapon to fight against the enemies who live and enjoy in injustice, in war, in hatred, in lies. As Paul clarifies remarkably that the reason for his intensive and enduring pursuit of carrying his own crosses like Jesus was to fill in what has been undone in Jesus's redemptive project,

> *Now I rejoice in my sufferings for your sake, and in my flesh I am filling up what is lacking in the afflictions of Christ on behalf of his body, which is the church.* (Col. 1:24)

In Jesus's days, the cross was a curse and sort of an electric chair. Consequently, the cross had its notorious and abominable identity of its own. But after Jesus used it, after he died on it, the same cross has become the symbol and source of salvation of humanity. The loss has become gain; the pain has produced joy; the death changed into life; and bleeding has turned out to be living waters. Describing the historical change that occurred in the identity of the cross, Pope St. Leo the Great said, "*The cross of Christ is the source of every blessing, the fountain of all merit; to the faithful it gives strength from His weakness, glory from His shame, and life from His death.*"

Undoubtedly, when we the merciful look up to him crucified on the cross, that dreadful sight makes us shed tears and mourn for him; we are moved to remorse of conscience, our hearts beat with longing to be like him in our CHESED undertakings—valiant, magnanimous, forgiving, well-balanced. Secondly, we start longing for his immense love and for living like him chivalrously and going beyond the boundaries, come what may, to those who are miserably weak, underdeveloped, hungry, and having been crucified sometimes lifelong in that miserable misery. The sight of our crucified Lord urged millions of saints and disciples to go for his love sake from country to country in consoling, in supporting, in healing the underdogs of the world. St. Teresa of Avila very well said, *"Desire earnestly always to suffer for God in everything and on every occasion."*

Jesus underwent all his sufferings with an ultimate aim of bestowing salvation to his fellowmen, plus demonstrating his total love for God and his human brothers and sisters. There have been in human history so many people who were edified by Jesus's cross-management and tried hard to follow his footsteps. They were convinced that only by this they can be true disciples of Jesus who invites all to follow him, not just stand by or behind the cross but take it up and accompany him. That is what Jesus preached, and that is what he lived. We also should keep in mind that not every suffering is salvific, but every suffering, even if it is a little ache and pain, can be a source of salvation to others if it is borne in communion with Jesus and with his intentions. Thomas A. Kempis writes in his book *Imitation of Christ*: *"He who knows how to suffer will enjoy much peace. Such a one is a conqueror of himself and lord of the world, a friend of Christ, and an heir of heaven."*

Mercy Is Not Justice Denied

Real life is very complex for Christians who seriously want to live out their faith in a sinful world. Friends who approach me for spiritual counseling put to me certain practical questions in this matter of the CHESED rare blending of mercy and justice: Can I be consistently merciful and yet be a parent who spanks my child for disobedience? Can I be consistently merciful and yet be an employer who pay good wages for the dutiful but dismiss irresponsible employees? Can I be consistently merciful and yet be a judge who give stiff penalties for drunk driving and child abuse? Can I be consistently merciful and yet be a pastor who follow the church's disciplinary tradition of excommunicating a church member for any public sin? The first and the only response I give to them is that it is God's will that as long as this age lasts, there will be this rare blend of mercy and justice in every dimension and sphere of earthly life.

In the Good Book of Jesus, we discover justice as something that should be practiced along with mercy and faithfulness. They are not mutually exclusive. However, it is not impossible for us to act justly and be merciful. God in Jesus demonstrated this rare-blended performance. Nonetheless, it is an eternal truth that a proud person cannot uphold such divinely rare blend. The truth of God is, only a humble heart that is melted in God's powerful furnace of mercy can practice administering justice with a heart of mercy. When we walk humbly with God, we are able to act justly, at the same time being merciful.

CHESED Deeds in My Priestly Life

In every homily, I never conclude it without a personal testimony from my life. Hence in this book also, let me end it with a testimony about how and why I as a priest should live a CHESED-oriented life in order to get my heavenly crown of the blessed.

Pope Francis, from the first day of his pontificate till this day, has made priests like me to revisit and reorientate and renew my priestly responsibility of accomplishing merciful acts and lead a CHESED-oriented ministry. Very fortunately, Pope Francis has been inspired by the Spirit of Jesus to include regular references on this matter in all of his daily homilies, public talks, and surely very elaborately in his writings. I have collected most of his sayings and saved them in my computer to help me in my daily prayer and meditation, especially during this Year of Mercy. In one of his addresses during a general audience (Ref. Zenit. com 11-12-14), he spoke in detail what the scriptures and the church say on the ministries of church leaders, like bishops, priests, deacons, and so on.

Referring to Paul's pastoral letters to Timothy and Titus, the pope underlined the basic grammar of every ministry in the Church:

> *Now, it is emblematic how, together with the gifts inherent in the faith and in the spiritual life, that can't be overlooked in that very life, some exquisitely human qualities are listed: hospitality, sobriety, patience, meekness, reliability and goodness of heart. I repeat: hospitality, sobriety, patience, meekness, reliability and goodness of heart. This is the alphabet, the basic grammar of every ministry! It should be the basic grammar of every bishop, of every priest and of every deacon!*

> *Yes, because without this good and genuine predisposition to encounter, to know, to dialogue, to appreciate and relate with ones brethren in a respectful and sincere way, it is not possible to offer a truly joyous and reliable service and witness.*

The pope, who is appointed by the mercy of God to be an inspiration to all the merciful, added his thoughts on the underlying merciful attitude that every bishop, priest, and deacon should possess in their love ministries. Indicating what Paul writes in his letter to Timothy (1 Tim. 4:14; 2 Tim. 1:6), he taught,

> *The Apostle exhorts to revive continually the gift that was received. This means that the awareness must always be alive that one is not a Bishop, priest or deacon because one is more intelligent, good and better than others, but only because of a gift of love, a gift of God freely given, in the power of His Spirit, for the good of His people. This awareness is truly important and is a grace to pray for every day! In fact, a Pastor who is conscious that his ministry flows only from the mercy and heart of God will never be able to assume an authoritarian attitude, as if everyone was at his feet and the community was his property, his personal kingdom.*

As a human being, I consistently confess that I join the club of millions of disciples of Jesus—the laity, theologians, saints, sages, and leaders—who struggle perennially to fathom the universalism of God's salvation. It is a mystery by itself. Even after thoroughly searching for the right meaning of God's CHESED as proclaimed both in scriptures and church tradition, I humbly acknowledge my personal deficiency in getting the depth of this mystery. I am in agony to understand and explicate fully the in-depth theology and application of God's rare-blended justice and mercy in his economy of salvation. Such a struggle and tension is not just in me. It has been exposed even in Paul's writings.

Starting from the teachings and writings of Clement of Alexandria, Gregory of Nyssa, Theodore of Mopsuestia, and Gregory Nazianzen and going through theologians like St. Thomas Aquinas who, indicating the rare blend of CHESED in God's realm, first made the claim that the virtue of hope, based on faith and nourished by love, would open up salvation not only for oneself but for all universally, many of the theologians in this era such as Hans Urs von Balthasar, Karl Barth, and Hans Küng, who have tried their best in expounding the doctrinal faith on universal salvation for all, blended with God's justice to be done at the end for the evil forces, finally came to a humble conclusion,echoing the words of Josef Pieper in his little treatise on hope:

> Only hope is able to comprehend the reality of God that surpasses all antitheses, to know that his mercy is identical with his justice and his justice with his mercy.

This is where I stand rowing my lifeboat of Catholic faith. I cannot say or do personally anything about God's rare blend of justice and mercy. I am convinced that because of my human weakness and frailty, I can neither go with the flow nor can I swim against the current of the immensity of God's CHESED. The only thing I would be doing is, hoping with hope in the incredible mercy of God, but always trembling in fear for the truthful justice of the same God, I will do the merciful deeds as my church suggests to me, with open arms.

Let me end my book with the beautiful words of Blessed Mother Teresa, as posted by one of my friends in Facebook on December 13, 2015:

- *People are often unreasonable and self-centered. Forgive them anyway.*
- *If you are kind, people may accuse you of ulterior motives. Be kind anyway.*
- *If you are honest, people may cheat you. Be honest anyway.*
- *If you find happiness, people may be jealous. Be happy anyway.*
- *The good you do today may be forgotten tomorrow. Do good anyway.*
- *Give the world the best you have, and it may never be enough. Give your best anyway.*
- *For you see in the end, it is between you and God. It was never between you and them.*

This is my manifesto for all that I accomplish in my ministries of mercy and justice.

I also want to add one more point to this manifesto: I am merciful because ultimately I want to be crowned with the blessedness from my Master.

Other books by Rev. Benjamin A. Vima

SONDAY SONRISE: Sunday Homilies for three Liturgical Years

DAILY DOSE for Christian Survival: Daily Scriptural Meditations and Spiritual Medication

PRAYERFULLY YOURS: Qualityprayer for Qualitylife

CATHOLIC CHRISTIAN SPIRITUALITY for New Age Dummies

MY RELIGION: REEL OR REAL? A Postmodern Catholic's Assessment of his religion

MINISTRY IN TEARS: International Priests' missionary Life & Ministry (Co-authored by his brother Rev. Dasan Vima, SJ)

HILLTOP MEDITATIONS for Year C weekend Spiritual Nourishment

Printed in the United States
By Bookmasters